The House of the Lord
Stories from the Family Room

Phyllis Calvey

Illustrations by Brian Calvey

Sheed & Ward

Sheed & Ward™ is a service of The National Catholic Reporter Publishing Company.

Library of Congress Catalog Card Number: 92-64036

ISBN: 1-55612-550-X

Published by: Sheed & Ward
115 E. Armour Blvd.
P.O. Box 419492
Kansas City, MO 64141-6492

To order, call: (800) 333-7373

Contents

To my sister Mary
who has held my hand since we were little

Acknowledgements

To our children, Trevor and Jessie, who wrote so many of these stories through the very living of their lives. They were our eyes to see the richness and light church gives to family.

To my very dear father and mother whose house belongs to us, the children. And to my sisters and brothers who taught me about the love and strength of family.

To our Pastor, Rev. James Connolly, who showed us The House of The Lord, too, belongs to the children. And through his insight and wisdomthe children who live there are encouraged to "grow."

To our sisters and brothers at St. Blaise who share this house with us. It is they who have given us such a wonderful view of the "family room."

from Phyllis and Brian Calvey
two who love God joined as one

Introduction

I still refer to it as "my house," even though I moved out years ago and now have a house of my own. The truth of the matter is, a house always belongs to the children who grew up in it.

The family room is the center where it all takes place; the forming and bonding of different children born to the same family. Ordinary children, like the utensils in a kitchen drawer, never intended to be the same. Each one designed to serve the family in his/her own way.

The spirit-filled parish of the 90s is not unlike the base communities in the Third World. Believers gather to hear together Jesus' words. They hear Jesus speaking within the ordinary circumstances of life as they are living it. Stories carry truth and are open-ended. They reach directly into people's lives.

Stories, to me, seem a natural way of sharing the experience of the church family. After all, Jesus made us one large family when He taught us to pray by saying Our Father. And how can we pray, Our Father, unless we see every child of His as our brother and sister?

The House of the Lord belongs to the children who grew up there. Children intended to be different; each one with his/her own special gift to return to the family of God.

The House of the Lord offers a view from the family room, as seen by one of the children.

"I Will Dwell in the House of the Lord
All the Days of My Life."

—23rd Psalm—

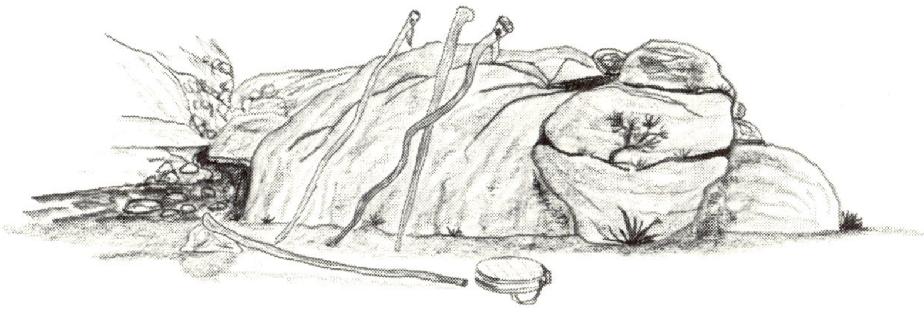

Keep Going—It's Worth the Effort!

TODAY HAD TO BE THE PRETTIEST SUNDAY OF THE YEAR. They were here at last, driving up to the gate of one of the most climbed mountains in New England, Mt. Monadnock in New Hampshire. The attendant handed them a map of the mountain. "Just want to let you folks know that it's a good three and a half hour climb to the mountain's summit." He subconsciously looked at his watch as he directed them to the parking area. They bought drumsticks at the refreshment stand and sat at the picnic tables under the pines. "No matter which trail we choose," he said looking at the map, "there's no getting out of the fact that it's a three and a half hour climb to the top. It's noon already." "I know we can make it in less time than that," his wife replied. "The kids are used to walking in the woods." Both of the children begged to go. So he carefully selected a smooth walking stick for each of them.

The first steps of the trail opened to a wonderland. Giant trees touched to form a perfect multi-colored roof over a carpet of pine needles and soft earth. "This isn't so hard," she said and quickened the pace. But twenty minutes later the path changed to steep steps made from whole trees that had been placed like stair treads to keep the earth from washing away. After an hour of climbing up each one with such determined effort, they felt positive they were making great time. "How far are we from the top?" she called out to three young men who were on their way down. "I'd say you're one quarter of the way to the tree line," one of the men answered. "It's another hour from there to the summit." "One quarter of the way just to the tree line," she repeated. "There's a cold spring just around the next bend," he added. "Which trail is the fastest way to the summit?" her husband asked. "We've done both," he replied. "I would definitely say White Cross is better on the way up and White Dot on the way down. If you look at the map White Cross looks longer, but it's an easier climb for the kids, and you make up the time with the faster pace." Before he continued on his way he looked at them and smiled. "Keep going," he said, "it's worth the effort!"

In a matter of minutes they heard the rushing water of the spring. Rounding the bend, they saw the old-fashioned wooden bridge which edged the stream where a huge pipe of clear mountain water was emptying into. Another climber was rinsing and refilling his water canteens. "Next time we'll have to bring a water jug," the husband said. They drank long and splashed the cold water on their hot necks and arms. They rested on the big logs watching the people as they drank and studied the map, trying to decide which trail to take. "To the mountain!" she called pointing her walking stick toward the sky.

Every so often they would ask the people coming down how much further it was to the tree line. They were pretty sure how far it was, but they loved hearing the words that each climber said: "Keep going, it's worth the effort!" The last stretch was the hardest. The climb was straight up the rocks. But finally they could see blotches of sunlight and feel a drastic change in the air. They climbed right out of the trees and the whole forest opened up to an enormous blue sky. Talk about seeing the forest from the trees!

They sat on some long flat rocks. From there they had a clear view of the trails below and the summit above. Though the climb had seemed like a straight climb up, now they could see it was more of a windy one. Some of the paths went around and around the mountain with no way up to the top. They watched the many families making their way up the paths. Some were half way. Some a little further. One family was no more than a ten minute climb from breaking the tree line. They were turning around to go back. They had no idea what lay just a little ahead.

"How far to the summit?" the husband asked as some people came by. It looked so close now. "It's about an hour away," they answered. "But from this point on the climbing is easy. You hardly notice you're even climbing. There's white dots painted on the stones that mark the trail from this point on."

They were still debating whether or not to continue. Suddenly a little girl no more than five popped out of the trees. Her face was radiant when she saw the distance she had climbed. "Do you think you can make it all the way up there?" her father asked. He pointed to the peak that lay ahead. "It's still a long way to walk." Without a word she put her small hand in his and turned toward the peak. "That's my little girl," he said proudly, and they disappeared into the bushes.

"And a child shall lead them," she said. "Let's follow the yellow brick road." They picked up their walking sticks. Just like they were told, white dots were painted on the stones ahead. They made the journey much easier. Imagine the man who had to decide where all people to come after him would step, she thought. As they reached the last step up the mountain the people there began clapping for them. "You made it," they exclaimed and shook their hands. Suddenly they found themselves jumping and waving too. "We made it!" they exclaimed. "We didn't turn back."

Surprisingly the climb down was even harder on the legs than on the way up. Yet, it had an excitement all its own. Now they were the ones telling how far it was to the tree line. They were giving advice about the trails and telling about the cold springs they had found. And to every climber they passed, they took time to say, "keep going—it's worth the effort!"

At the very bottom of the mountain they met a lovely lady who was just beginning the climb. It was almost dark.

Something in her step told them it wasn't her first encounter with the mountain. She looked at the four of them, letting a sparkle come into her eyes, and said, "Am I almost there?"

The ride home was peaceful. She looked at her sleepy children in the back seat and a wonderful awareness filled her. They were climbing another mountain together; the highest mountain of all—the mountain of the Lord's house. She knew it wouldn't be an easy climb. When the road got rough there would always be that temptation to turn back. But there would be springs too, she thought. And people who would stop to encourage them along the way. They had a wonderful guide who had already given their family a map of God's mountain. She could see clearly what her task was. She had to get her children above the tree line before they went out on their own. She wanted to get them to the flat rocks so they could see the paths they had climbed. From that point they would have a clear view of the summit that lay in the distance. A vision so beautiful that they would spend the rest of their lives climbing toward it. She closed her eyes and prayed.

Come, let us climb the Lord's mountain,
to the house of the God of Jacob,
That he may instruct us in his ways,
and we may walk in his paths.

Mea Culpa, Mea Culpa, Mea Maxima Culpa

EVERYWHERE YOU LOOKED THE COUNTDOWN WAS BEING announced: 16 days left until Christmas. Of course they meant shopping days. She refused to allow Christmas to become a blur of shopping for presents. She looked forward to the beautiful Christmas Penitential Celebration her church offered the Monday before Christmas week. This put everything in perspective. The Penitential was more than a family tradition. The children knew that there was no celebrating Christmas without it.

The four of them drove into the church parking lot at seven. It was a typical cold, dark too-early December evening. The church was inviting. On this night it was lit in the warm glow of candlelight.

As they entered the church she directed her son and daughter to a bench in the back. Her husband sat beside her. When they were seated, she handed each of them a pencil and a piece of small paper that was at the end of all the benches. Before they went to confession, everyone wrote down a sin they would like to have burned. Then, they dropped the paper in a huge urn in the front of the church on their way to the priest. After they made their confession, they received a small white candle with cardboard around it to keep the wax from dripping on your hand.

She wanted this to be a perfect night, one in which she felt pure and free from sin. It took a long time to decide what sin to write on the paper. That now accomplished, she spent the rest of the time carefully going over the "list" of sins she had memorized, and now was mentally checking off to make sure she wasn't forgetting any. Her eyes were glued to the crucifix. She was ready.

The homily was about social sins. Father was saying something about sin being more what we fail to do. But it was hard to concentrate on what he was saying and remember the list of sins at the same time. Before long, two priests went in the confessionals. Three other priests were hearing confessions face to face.

Then something happened for which she was totally unprepared. There was a slide projector set up and suddenly slides were being shown on the large wall where the cross hung. Music was playing softly in the background. The first slide showed an elderly woman staring blankly out her apartment window. The woman had tears in her eyes. The old woman's pain and loneliness seeped into the church.

An episode in the supermarket that she had long forgotten popped into her mind. An elderly man in the bakery section had held up a loaf of bread and asked her how much it was. She could still see his face. The look in his eyes hadn't escaped her. She had been in such a hurry that day. She remembered how she strategically turned her grocery carriage so she could tell him the price as she looked over her shoulder. Tears stung her eyes.

The second slide was the scene of a run-down tenement. Children playing amidst the litter and broken glass. Next, a picture of the homeless sleeping on air vents, huddled near buildings trying to block the wind. And in the background of each slide our cross on the church wall was plainly visible.

Slowly, the list of sins crumbled in her mind as she began to understand the words Father had spoken. Perhaps it isn't the sins we do that need confessing. We need to look at what we don't do. When we turn our backs on the homeless, the poor, the lonely, that too is sin.

For the first time that evening she became aware of the people sitting in church with her. Most heads were bent in prayer. Their faces reflected such sorrow and remorse. She wondered what filled their hearts tonight. Were they hurting? What was their pain? For one brief moment she thought she was going to stand up and reach out to them. She wanted to ask their forgiveness first before she went to confession.

"Forgive me," she whispered. "Forgive me for what I've done to hurt you. But more than that, forgive me for what I haven't done when you needed me."

She took another piece of paper and began to write a new message. She placed her paper in the urn and eagerly went up to say her confession. This time she was not only filled with peace, but with the feeling of promise. When the priest lit their "past" on fire, she felt a new fire slowly begin within her. From that fire Father lit the candles people were holding at each end of the bench. And they, in turn, lit their neighbor's candles. She had never thought of the symbol of the light before that evening. That each person should bring his/her light to another until the whole world was filled with light, the light of Christ.

Then came the finale. They sang Joy to the World with all their heart while bells were rung from every direction in the church.

She felt so alive, so fresh, so new. She wished for some way to express the wonder of it all. When they walked out of church it was snowing.

Waiting by the Window

I WOULD SAY THAT LITTLE GIRL WAS JUST ABOUT YOUR AGE. She had the same sparkly eyes and that cute little upturned nose. She was a lot like you, too, except that instead of getting excited at this time of year, she got sad. Her father was out of work. And there are no jobs in Appalachia where she lives now that the coal mines have shut down. With four sisters and four brothers in the family, no one dared even think about Christmas coming.

But one Sunday at Church everything changed. The little girl had heard the words with her own ears, "Jesus is coming at the time you least expect." No one had to tell her what the word expect meant. Why her mother had been expecting a baby just last month. And she had waited and watched for that baby for the longest time. Then one morning her father said the baby came during the night. And all the people that visited said that most babies come during the middle of the night when no one is ready.

Well, she wasn't going to let that happen with the baby Jesus. So that very night, after everyone was asleep, she slipped out of bed and watched out the window. She planned to wait by the window every night until Christmas.

"I have a surprise," her mother said one night after supper. "We are all going out to the mission house." "But we never go out at night," the little girl said, thinking about the window. "Besides, we don't have warm coats and the four youngest have no shoes to wear." "We are going out tonight," her father said in a voice that told her it was of no use to argue about it. "We'll just have to carry the little ones." "And if we all hurry," her mother added, "I'll bet we can get there before the cold even knows we've left."

The little mission house was full of light. From every direction other families like hers were running to the welcoming door. The little girl's mouth fell open when she walked inside the large living room. The entire room was empty except for a manger filled with straw that was placed in the middle of the room. One by one families sat around it until all the families the little girl knew were there.

So much heat in an inside place in winter seemed strange. It made her eyelids blink. Her body was tingling and her legs were itchy from running. Before she knew what was happening, someone placed a coat in her lap. It must be a mistake, she thought. She looked around. Beautiful clothes were, being handed to everyone, even to the mothers and fathers. Scarves, hats, mittens, socks, sneakers and those bright colored shoelaces some of the city children have. Every child in the room was given a candy bar. There were coloring books and crayons besides. A group of boys were bouncing a basketball in the corner of the room. Then Sister stood near her smiling and holding out the prettiest dress she had ever seen. It was bluer than the bluest sky on a clear day.

"For me?" she said. "For me?" The whole room vanished as she held her little dress close to her. She was too excited to speak. She looked at her mother, wanting so much to know what was happening.

"You see," her mother explained, "Sister told some people at a church far away about our little mission out here. And the people said they must send some boxes for Christmas. They gave things they had. The little girl who sent your coat and dress needed bigger ones."

The whole room was filled with the feeling that only comes at Christmas. Sister lit a candle and they all began to sing *Away in a Manger*. It was clear that the baby Jesus had come.

The little girl's eyes filled with tears. She suddenly remembered the words she had heard that Sunday in Church, "Jesus will come at the time you least expect . . . ."

The Christmas Bonus

WE WERE PROUD PARENTS WALKING INTO THE HALL THAT december afternoon. The principal spotted me in the crowd and came over. "You have a fine student there," he began. "First-place winner in our high school essay competition. I don't have to ask who he takes after." He shook hands with my son.

Then he turned to me kind of thoughtfully. "I read in the paper that your sister Elisha was recently promoted to a management position in her company. She really made it, didn't she? We all knew she was bright. And such a go-getter. There was really no doubt she'd make it big someday." He rubbed his chin. "If I recall, you were right behind her. I thought sure you would have made it, too, only in a quieter way." He smiled, kind of curious as to what happened.

"I did make it," I answered, much to his surprise. I looked directly at him. "I am exactly where I want to be."

Then I returned to my table.

He would never understand about being a pastoral minister. I ran programs as great as my sister directed. I developed new ideas. I made presentations to hundreds of people. Yet, people would never think of my job as "having made it big." And how could I expect him to understand? I didn't even want to admit to myself that I was feeling a little down over December. It's a hard thing to admit when you're surrounded by blessings.

Yet, in December everyone is talking of their Christmas bonus, of their review and pay increases. Two people in my family were celebrating Christmas bonuses of thousands, not hundreds, of dollars. I couldn't help but think how just their bonus, not even to mention their pay, would nearly pay for my son's college education in the fall. Perhaps there was a little envy, too, that people would never really think of me as successful.

Ever since the dinner, the principal's words stayed with me like a shadow. Even as I walked into our lovely church on Christmas Eve, they were there. We arrived early.

My husband was playing and singing for the Christmas Eve pageant. I was secretly thankful that all I had to do was distribute the music sheets. When my daughter and I finished, we sat quietly in our bench. Immediately, the words came again like a pesty mosquito buzzing in my ear: "I thought for sure you would have made it, too, only in a smaller way." I tried to pray.

To my surprise, one of the other mothers was coming toward me in our bench. She shyly handed me a woven basket. Inside was a white linen fringed cloth she had neatly embroidered. The bright red stitchery said, "Bread shared with friends makes any meal a feast." In the cloth was a little loaf of cranberry nut bread wrapped in bright tin foil and topped with a satin red ribbon.

"I don't have your way with words," she began, "but I wanted you to know you have always been there when I needed you. You will never know the difference you have made in our lives. But I wanted to give you this to let you know how I felt." Her eyes were misty. She gently hugged me and kissed my cheek.

"Thank you so very much," I whispered. She left to go back to her three young boys and her husband.

"What did she give you?" my daughter asked as she peeked in the basket. The answer came through the tears slipping down, "My Christmas bonus."

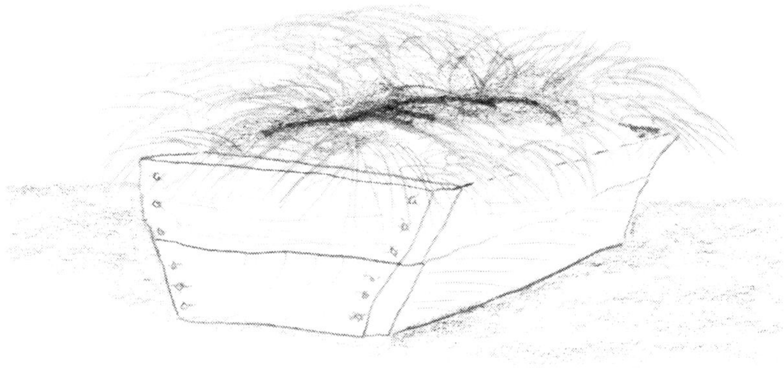

The Christmas Secret

DID YOU KNOW THERE IS A SECRET IN THE CHRISTMAS STORY?

A long time ago Mary and Joseph had to go back to the place where they were born because the king of the land wanted all the people to be counted. Joseph had a little donkey for Mary to ride because it was such a long way to go. When at last they arrived at the inn, the innkeeper said there was no room. He showed them a stable where he kept his animals and said they could rest there. The stable was warm and dry. Mary and Joseph were very tired and it was very late. So Joseph said they would stay there for the night. And there in the stable, in the night, the baby Jesus was born.

Mary wrapped her little baby boy in pieces of cloth, and they placed Him in a manger. What do you think a manger is?

Sometimes people picture it as a little cradle. Did you know that a manger is not a bed at all? A manger is a feed box. It is a place where food for the cows and donkeys and oxen was kept.

You know that Jesus is the son of Mary and Joseph. But you also know that Jesus is the Son of God. Because Jesus is God's Son, He could have come to us any way He wanted. He could have come to us in a cradle or a crib. He could have been placed in a small bed with warm quilts. Yet He chose to come to us in a manger, a box that food is placed in. He did that for a very special reason. In fact, it was His Christmas secret to us—that He was born to be *our* food. He told us that anyone who comes to Him will never be hungry.

Jesus knew that people would be hungry all of their life. People would be hungry not just for food, but for many things. People would be hungry for His word, for the truth, for love, for friends, for ways to make them happy. Because of the manger, we know that Jesus came to feed us in all the ways we are hungry.

Jesus had many secrets to tell us about why He came. But He knew He wouldn't always be here to tell us in person. So He had to find special ways, like the manger, to tell us His secrets.

Don't you think the manger is a very special Christmas secret?

The Rocking Chair

"WHAT DO YOU WANT FOR CHRISTMAS, MA?" HER LITTLE girl asked. "All I want is for you to be good," she answered. Her son came in from the other room. "Being good doesn't count as a present," he said. "Tell us something we can buy for you." She laughed. "Let me tell you about a Christmas when I was a young girl. It's a Christmas I'll never forget." Her two children sat down in the living room. They loved stories, especially stories from the past.

"I guess all mothers feel the same way," she said. "Because every year when we were little we asked my mother what she wanted for Christmas. And she always said the same thing. All she wanted was for us to be good. And just like you, it didn't seem like a big enough present back then."

"As kids, we never had much money. Every year we all chipped in and bought her the best gift we could afford. It never was very much. But that year my sister and I both had steady babysitting jobs. We were determined to save and buy her the rocking chair she said she'd someday have. The six of us saved from our allowance too. Even Gerry, who was four at the time, seemed to understand. He gave us some pennies from his piggy bank. By the time Christmas came we had saved $30.00. It was exactly enough to buy a rocking chair. We couldn't afford the one with flowers or stencils painted on. But nothing looked as grand to our young eyes as that rocking chair did. It took a lot of strategy to get it home without her knowing. But come Christmas Eve, that rocking chair was safely hidden upstairs in our room."

"We could hardly get to sleep at all that night. Six o'clock Christmas morning, we gathered in the bedroom and carried the rocking chair into the parlor. As we tiptoed into the room we tried not to peek at the presents Santa had left for us during the night. But there, almost in the middle of everything, stood the biggest bouncing horse I had ever seen. No one said a word about it. Little Gerry, who seemed the most excited, beat all of us into our parents' bedroom. He was tugging on my mother's hand, trying to get her up. 'All right, I'm coming,' she said. She knew how excited he must be about his wonderful surprise. She got out of bed and he took her hand. He led her right past the rocking horse and brought her beside the rocking chair. His bright brown eyes were shining with pride as he pointed to the chair and said, 'That's for you.'"

"She looked at him standing there in his yellow feet pajamas and realized that he was so excited about the present he had for her, that he never even noticed his own. It was the first time I had ever seen my mother cry. That was the year I learned what Christmas is all about; giving gifts that can't be bought."

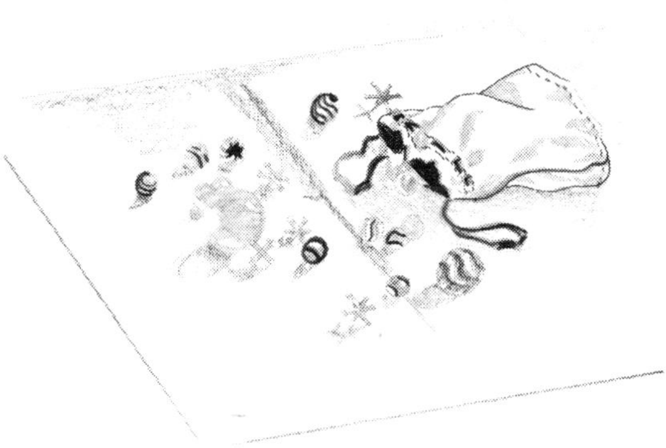

Meet Jesus of Nazareth

"WHAT WAS ABRAHAM LINCOLN'S MOTHER'S NAME?" I ASKED the kids. We had just finished reading a wonderful book called *Meet Abraham Lincoln*. The book told many interesting things about Lincoln's childhood. After I finished reading a book I always tested the kids' memory. It made them more attentive to the story. And they delighted in trying to answer all the questions I might ask. We enjoyed learning how different Lincoln's life was in the time he lived. Now when the children heard the name Abraham Lincoln, they had a real place to picture him in. They could see the log cabin he grew up in. They knew a little about his life and how his family lived. They knew the chores he did as a boy and loved the story how he walked miles to borrow a book to read. They also understood why he was called Honest Abe.

After we finished reading that book we looked through the others in the series: *Meet George Washington, Meet the Pilgrim Fathers, Meet John Adams;* the list was endless. Suddenly I thought how wonderful it would be if there were a book called *Meet Jesus of Nazareth.* It suddenly occurred to me how little we knew about the life of Jesus as a boy. At thirty, I still pictured him in the clouds.

We talked about it and decided to look for a book on Jesus' life when he was a boy. It took almost a month to find the right one. My son was too excited to wait until night for me to read it to them. He asked if he could read it himself. I was thrilled. He took the book out to the screenhouse. It wasn't before long that he was running through the side door of the house. "I can't believe it," he said. "All this time I couldn't figure out why people called Jesus the bread of life. Bread is such a common thing. I mean we just go to the store and buy it. It's nothing so special. And I really wondered why people back then would have chosen something that ordinary to call Jesus." "But Mom," he said, "You should see how hard it was to make bread when Jesus was a boy. Did you know that they didn't have ovens? Mary and Jesus had to gather brush to make a fire. Sometimes it took them all morning to find enough brush or thistle. Then Mary had to grind the wheat in a bowl using a stone to crush it. They didn't eat breakfast. They ate only two meals a day. For lunch, they ate bread and cheese and fruit and water. Only on special feasts did they have meat. I never really thought about Jesus being a little boy," he said. "But Jesus had chores to do just like me. I wonder if he had to go to school too." He grabbed an apple and walked out the side door, reading the book as he went.

I wondered too. I watched his curly blond head walk down the steps. This afternoon Jesus was coming out of the clouds!

This House Belongs to Them

"THERE'S NO PLACE LIKE HOME, EXCEPT MAYBE NANA and pepe's house," she said. When my children were little, I had the hardest time trying to teach them to knock on the door when we went to visit them. They would always race up the steps to their house, and no matter how often I reminded them, they rushed right in without knocking. Well, this particular day I was in the living room scolding them about it, when my father overheard. He called me over in a hurry. The kids just loved it. I don't think anything makes children happier than seeing their own parents get in trouble. My father told me in no uncertain terms that his grandchildren did not have to knock on the door at his house. I gently reminded him that this wasn't their house. He put an arm around each of my children, looked at me, and said, 'This house belongs to them.'" "I thought about that for a long time. You know, he's right. My son can go to Nana's anytime and he knows she'll have honeybuns in the freezer, simply because that's his favorite snack. And there'll be dried fruit and gum in one of the cupboards for my daughter. Even the littlest grandchild knows where his 'quackers' are. All of the grandchildren know about the little brown teapot with the orange berry flowers. Each of them has had their first cup of coffee from that little teapot. One spoon of coffee and the rest milk, but real coffee nonetheless. A pink spoon and cup belongs to the set, and all morning if they want to, they can spoon coffee out of the teapot into their own special cup. It doesn't matter that they spill most of it. Nana doesn't mind. They sit on her lap and kiss her and spill and she keeps a cloth in her hand just for that purpose.

Anyone looking would think the bureau in Nana's bedroom was just an ordinary bureau. But the grandchildren know differently. They know the third drawer is a magic drawer. It holds large pocketbooks to play postman or doctor or dress up. There are countless other treasures and new surprises that mysteriously find their way into the drawer. They can play pretend and be anything they want to be at Nana's house. My father was right when he said that house belongs to them.

I didn't see it all so clearly until my sister moved away, to Japan, in fact. She was expecting her first child when her husband lost his job. He received a great offer teaching English as a foreign language. So off they moved to Japan. They planned to visit often. One thing led to another and it was years before they could manage a trip home. They were expected to arrive on Christmas Eve. The whole family, including all the grandchildren, gathered at Nana and Pepe's to see their little cousin for the first time. I remember watching in the window. At last their car pulled in the driveway. Their little girl came up the steps and we heard a timid knock on the door. Nana quickly opened it, but still she wouldn't come in. Her parents brought her in the house and Nana reached down to pick her up. I guess it was overwhelming to see so many people at one time. She started crying and tried to hide behind her mother. Her mother kept saying, go see Nana, but the truth of the matter was, Nana was a stranger. She had heard about Nana since she was a baby. She knew many stories about Nana's house, but Nana was still a stranger.

They stayed for two weeks and all that time I felt a sadness for the little girl. She had missed the carefree days of spilling from the little orange berry teapot. The bureau in Nana's room looked like any other bureau. Her eyes didn't see the magic in the drawer. She didn't know where to hang the Christmas stockings. That house didn't belong to her.

They returned to Japan, and in time I put the incident out of my mind until something happened to bring it all back.

My husband and I were asked to help with the First Communion program at our church. It's a wonderful program. On one of the preparation nights, the parents and the children meet in church to experience church hands-on. During the course of the evening, the children baptize 5 dolls. They try on the priest's clothes and learn what all the colors mean. They go in and out of the confessional box, and listen to a story about forgiveness. They play a community game to learn about trust. They set the altar table, and talk about Eucharist as a meal they share with friends. They get to taste the bread for the very first time in their life.

My husband and I were in charge of the altar table. We were sitting up on the altar while the First Communion teacher was explaining how they would separate into five groups: A, B, C, D, E. Each group was given 20 minutes at each different station set up in church. We were station A, the altar table. When the teacher said it was time to begin, I watched the children's reaction. Half of the children ran to their assigned place. The other half shyly hid behind their mother's leg. Their parents had to physically take their hand and almost drag them up. I overheard some of the parents saying, "What's the matter with you, why can't you be like the other boys and girls? They're not acting like that. Now you go up there like you're supposed to."

There was too much going on at the time to analyze what was happening, but each group that came up was the same. Half of the children were eager and excited, raising their hands to answer questions and asking if it was time to set the table yet. The other half were withdrawn and had a look of confusion about them. "What was all this about?," their faces seemed to say.

Later that evening, in the quiet of home, it all became clear. My sister's little girl came to mind. You see, half of the children's parents had moved away. The other half were children who visited once a week. This house, the Lord's house, belonged to them. They knew how to set the table. They had watched the Baptisms on Sunday morning. When they were infants, they watched as their mothers received something in her hand that must have been precious indeed the way she held it. When they were two and three, she took them by the hand when she went to receive that little white bread. And for years they were told that soon they would be big enough to receive Jesus themselves. Finally, that day had arrived. Yes, they were excited and eager. They ran up. This house belongs to them.

The other children, the ones who hid behind their parents, they were the ones whose parents decided to move away. Oh, their parents planned to visit often. But one thing always led to another. Now their children were seven, and it was their first visit back since they were born. They were the children who timidly knocked on the door to their Father's House, for His House did not belong to them.

The Sacrament of Baptism is a promise. A promise that you will come and visit once a week. It is seeing to it that this House, the House of the Lord, belongs to your children.

Dad Doesn't

THERE WERE SEVERAL FATHERS AT THE BAPTISM PREPARAtion class. Some were not too thrilled about being there. A woman stood up to speak. "This class is not to tell anyone how they should live their life. It is simply a sharing. My two children are teenagers. They are on their way out. Yours are just beginning their life with you. Believe me, things look very different from where I stand. I would like, in particular, to share a story with the fathers who are here this evening." All eyes immediately focus on the floor. She continues. "My son was thirteen when he suddenly stopped answering the prayers in church out loud. I always encouraged the children not to be shy about their faith. I always responded loudly to the prayers, and I expected them to do the same. When I asked him why he had stopped saying his prayers out loud, he was quick to answer, "Dad doesn't." I said, "I know Dad doesn't, but I do." He only repeated, "But Dad doesn't." My husband is quiet and never says his prayers for others to hear. He is a musician and music is his words. Thankfully, since that time, he has begun a church music ministry and leads our folk group. It took a little time to see through what my son was saying. He was saying, I'll do what my father does. How does my father respond to God? Does my father need church? How does a man find Jesus? It was natural for him to do this. After all, my husband was his role model for everything else, why not church? Children never learn what you tell them. That would be too easy. They learn by watching how you live your life. You can tell them over and over again how important it is that they go to church. Yet, if you don't go, what they're learning is that church is not important. If you have a daughter, you still don't get off the hook. You are her role model for the way her future family will pray. When she marries, if her father went to church with her, she will look to her husband to do the same. She will understand church as a family commitment. No one should force you to go to church. Yet, you must be aware that your life is a model for your children. I can honestly say that if my husband didn't go to church, my son would have stopped going at 15. In a two parent household, the son follows his father's path, especially if he can use it to his advantage.

They say life begins at 40. I believe it. My husband and I are on a second honeymoon. My own life is exciting. I have more time to do new and challenging things. In fact, I can do anything I choose. Anything, except for one thing. I can never change what I gave my children. I can't say, come back, there's something I forgot to tell you. When they were born, I thought that education would be our greatest gift to them. I was wrong. Giving them Jesus, giving them church in their lives, is the greatest gift we have given them. So many teenagers walk in a world of darkness, a world of despair. Part of the reason is their parents have forgotten the importance of "The Light" in their life. They had Jesus in their lives through their own childhood. But how do they expect their children to develop a relationship with Him? One day, each of us will meet our Maker. What excuse will be great enough to say, I'm sorry, I never brought my children to You. There is no other way for a child to know Jesus, except through their parents. Do you consider that to be one of your responsibilities as a parent?

Baptism is saying you will be the first teacher of your children in the ways of faith. Please don't teach them to say, "Daddy Doesn't."

Unless You Become Like Children

AGATHA WAS THERE FOR CONFESSION. SHE SAT IN THE bench, her eyes focused on the front of the altar. She recited her prayers. The priest spoke about the new spirit of the sacrament of Reconciliation. "This year," he said, "a few of our people will share some of their thoughts on the sacrament." Agatha was not a bit pleased. She was there for confession.

The priest introduced Miriam. Agatha recognized her from Sunday Mass. Nice enough woman, Agatha thought to herself. But I'm not here to listen to her. She continued to recite her rosary half aloud.

"Since our two children are only a year apart in school," Miriam began, "we decided to let them make their First Confession together. Also, it seemed more of a total family commitment this way." Miriam had such a pleasant speaking voice and easy way about her that Agatha found herself listening to her in spite of herself. Miriam continued.

"My daughter is more verbal in her feelings than my son, and the night of their First Confession, she looked at me quite seriously and said she had decided to turn her life around. I had to hide a smile for she had little to turn around. Yet, I was touched by how deeply this Sacrament had affected her.

She made her confession first and sat quietly near me in the pew. Suddenly she leaned close and whispered, "Father said for my penance I should do something nice for someone. I want this to be very, very special. What do you think I could do?" she asked.

I thought about it for a while and said, "Well, it is always easy to be nice to someone who is nice to you, and besides, you are already nice to everyone you meet. Why don't you decide to be nice to your brother when he makes you angry?"

"Ma," she said, "*That* won't work."

"Why not?" I asked.

"Because he is making his First Confession, too."

"So?" I asked, still missing her point.

"So, he won't be doing anything to make me angry anymore." And she looked surprised that I hadn't already thought of this. She turned again to face the altar. She folded her small hands in prayer.

What innocence, I thought, with a knowing smile. But as I studied her, the realization of what she had said struck me. I come here for confession and it's me and Jesus. I never stop to consider how other people are feeling. How they too are struggling and trying to change just as hard as I am. I never believe in them, really. I never take the time to wipe their slate clean, only my own.

For the first time in my life, I turned to look at the people sitting around me in church. They were so full of contrition. It was written so plainly on their faces while they prayed. The Sacrament of Penance is not a vertical Sacrament, heaven to me. It is more a horizontal Sacrament, arms and hearts extending out to all my brothers and sisters before reaching up to Jesus.

"Forgive me," I whispered, not to Jesus, but to them. "Forgive me my trespasses as I forgive you." A wonderful feeling swept over me. I realized that they did forgive me. They accepted me with all of my faults and weaknesses. I felt the power of the family of God. It felt different going to Jesus this way, receiving the Sacrament of Reconciliation with the "eyes" and the heart of a little child.

Miriam smiled and sat back down in her bench. In a few minutes people began going to confession. As Agatha got up to take her turn, she walked past Miriam. She stopped for a moment to gently place her hand across Miriam's shoulder. Agatha was trembling. She had never reached out to anyone in church before. Miriam looked up into her moist gray eyes. They exchanged so much more than a smile.

You see, though Agatha was there for confession, she received the Sacrament of Reconciliation.

The One Who Did the Father's Will

THERE IS A WONDERFUL CONNECTION BETWEEN THE FOOD on the table, the grain in the field and the cow in the pasture. Between the winter and dried apples, the summer and tomatoes. Between the preparation of a meal and the experience of love. Oftentimes, these basic connections are lost in our complex modern world.

The beginning of 1990, for many of our church families, was a time to rediscover some basic connections. The signs of the time are rising prices, unsure futures and a general feeling of recession. Yet, our community voted not only to continue, but to increase all of our monthly tithes for the coming year, while continuing to support the ones we give to on a yearly basis. I was given the privilege of writing the letters telling of the Good News that was to follow, news spoken through action, not words. The response from the missions we tithe to was near shock!

"How can this possibly be?" they wrote back. "In every direction we turn, our funds are being cut. People are afraid. They're looking for ways to tighten up, and the poor are usually the ones who lose. What makes you so different?" they wanted to know. "Surely things can't be better there than in the rest of the world."

We could write back and say it's a matter of trust, and that's the truth. Yet, it has more to do with the message in Matthew's Gospel. Jesus asked the chief priests and Jewish elders in the Temple, "But what is your opinion about this? There was a man with two sons. He went to the first and said, 'Go and work in my vineyard today, my son.' He said, 'I won't!' But afterwards he changed his mind and went. Then the father approached the second son with the same request. He said, 'All right, sir'—but he never went. Which of these two did what his father wanted?"

We no longer believe that attending Mass is saying yes to the Lord if we leave here and never do what He asks us to do in Memory of Him. The fact is, most times we are the second son in the story. We hear the Word on Sunday and our first response is no. After all, we wouldn't be real children if we said yes without a struggle. And like all parents, Jesus never expects easy things; He takes us right to the Mountain. So we go home and think about the kind of Father He's been to us, and think of what it means to be His sons and daughters, and so we change our minds.

In the end we become the child who does the Father's will. His will is for us to be with the poor. Give to your brothers and sisters when they are in need, He says again and again.

Perhaps we would all agree that the time for families to give what's left over is past. Now the decision is more: families giving up strawberries in December so that others can have them in June. We are called to sacrificial living. This simply means we choose to give back a part of all that was given to us. Each week, without fail, we make a planned return gift to Our Lord, not from what's left over, but from what was given to us. Many families have joined in this sacrificial giving experience. They said yes to the Lord with their lives, not with words. Only you can answer that important question: Will you go out and work in the vineyard today?

Last Christmas we all had our trees filled with presents for our own families. But there was a special present under the tree as well—our return gift to the Lord. And on Christmas morning while our own children excitedly opened their Christmas presents, another family in Haiti was opening their present from us. They wrote to tell us about it. On Christmas morning the family planned a procession. The mother, father and four children got up early, and singing their praises to the Lord, they carried their bug infested straw mattresses to be burned at the dump. For the first time in their lives, they could each have, for their very own, a dry cotton mattress. They could not believe they would ever live to see such a rich Christmas as this!

Tithing brings us back to the basic connections that are sometimes obscured in our complex modern world. The connection between the food on our Eucharistic table and the poor of the world. Between our wants and our needs. Between the sharing of the bread and the experience of Christ's love.

Tithing brings us back to being the child who does the Father's Will.

Bless Me

"I'M GOING TO DO IT ANYWAY AND YOU CAN'T STOP ME!" HE said as he stormed up to his room kicking and throwing things. Mumbled words that sounded like "I hate this whole family" and "I wish I could leave" brought clenched teeth in the living room as we tried to hold our tempers.

"Just stop it!" I yelled. "I don't want to hear another word!" He kicked the wall and flung himself on his bed. This was so unlike him. As a child he never threw a tantrum, now at fourteen he's starting.

Soon the house was quiet. I went to bed but couldn't sleep. He's such a good boy, I thought. How I wanted to go to him and talk it out. But we couldn't let him do what he wanted. He was frustrated. He was rebelling, trying to find himself. There were no answers, only pain.

Some time passed and I was sure he was asleep. What is he really thinking? I wondered. Slowly I began to picture him when he was a little boy and my mind was filled with his growing up. We have such a short time together. Why does it have to be so complicated, so pulled apart?

Suddenly my thoughts were broken as I heard footsteps coming down the stairs. I listened closer, yes, they belonged to Trevor. I waited to see if he was going to the bathroom. No. He turned in our room without a word and sat on my side of the bed. I waited. After a minute he said, "Bless me," in a very angry voice. Slowly he bent down so I could reach him and I touched his forehead and heard myself say the words I said each night. "Bless you, Trevor, in the Name of the Father, the Son, and the Holy Spirit." But this night was the first night I really "heard" the words, heard what they meant.

After the blessing my hand slid to Trevor's cheek and held it briefly.

"Is it okay?" was all he said.

"Yes," I answered, "It's okay." He went up to bed.

I lay in bed a long time thinking. I smiled. A simple tradition, so I thought. Each night the children said the same words, goodnight and bless me, almost as if they were one word. And each night, because of the blessing, our family went to bed at peace with God and one another.

His Will Be Done

MANY SUNDAYS THE PRIEST SPOKE ABOUT TAKING A RISK. God would take care of the rest, he assured them. Well, let's see if he's right, she thought. That Sunday she was taking the entire children's choir, thirty children in all, to sing at a local nursing home. She wouldn't have been so nervous if her own voice was stronger. She was counting on the priest's words to be true—God will take care of the rest.

When they arrived at the nursing home, they were ushered into a beautiful, large sitting room. Many patients were brought in by wheelchair.

The first part of the concert was arranged like the Mass itself. The entrance song went quite well. She then explained how they had a tradition of holding hands during the singing of the *Our Father.* The children spread out and took the hands of the people. They exchanged the sign of peace while they sang the song. The children happily shook hands with everyone. Some of the little ones reached out and tenderly touched the twisted feet and crippled hands that lay captive in the wheelchair.

The second part of the concert was a medley of Christmas songs. The guitar played the introduction and for some strange reason she couldn't find the note to begin the song. The guitar played the introduction twice more. Finally the children started the song by themselves, in a completely different key from the guitar. She lost control at that point and the entire medley was sung off key. Her face grew redder and redder by the minute. She was completely embarrassed. She couldn't wait to be out of there.

Once in the safety of her home, she vowed she would never put herself in a situation like that again. She had failed. The day had been a disaster; quite a humiliating experience. Her face turned red again just at the thought of it.

Three weeks later she received a note from the activities coordinator. The letter thanked her and said it had been one of the loveliest days the residents had known. They had been genuinely moved by the children. They were still talking about that wonderful afternoon. When could they come back?

She held the letter close to her. A blush rose to her cheeks. She had been so concerned about the music that she had missed the real reason they were there. The words rushed into her mind. Take a chance and God will take care of the rest. How foolish she was to think it meant that things would go according to her limited vision. A veil seemed to lift from her eyes. She could see the day clearly for the first time. The faces of the elderly coming to life, glowing at the touch of holding those little hands. She saw the soft smiles, the gentle eyes. A blush rose to her cheeks again. But for a different reason this time. The blush came from knowing that she took a chance, and He took care of the rest.

He Was Glad He Wasn't a Camel

THE DONKEY LIVED IN NAZARETH, A LITTLE TOWN IN galilee. And this day he heard talk of a census that would bring about great travel. Perhaps someone would ride him, he imagined. Then he could experience a great adventure that would carry him to unknown, exciting places. All of his life he dreamed of carrying someone important. Yet, he knew important men were rich enough to afford camels. Never mind, he thought, perhaps the census would take him in the presence of important people.

He was hired to go to Bethlehem. The couple was poor. The man was called Joseph, and his wife was named Mary. She was with child. It was a long journey. The donkey's short steps made the journey seem even longer. How he wished he had the long legs of a camel. But he did his very best. They made it in spite of the lions, wolves and bands of robbers that lived in the hills and were a threat to all travelers. At last, they arrived in Bethlehem.

The donkey's heart beat faster as Joseph went to the inn. Now the excitement would begin. The donkey would hear stories of greatness and meet important people. He couldn't believe the words Joseph was saying to Mary, "There is no room for us at the inn." The donkey's head hung in bitter disappointment as Joseph led him away from all the wonder the town had to offer. Away from all the rich people and the gaiety. Farther and farther they walked from the bustling noise of the crowd until they came to an almost hidden limestone cave. The cave was dark and extremely cold. It was barren except for some straw scattered here and there. The donkey spotted a manger standing in the corner. At least it would offer some protection when the baby came, he thought. The little donkey was kind. Seeing the cold cave made him determined to forget about himself and think of this poor couple. Perhaps he could help to bring some warmth into the cave for them.

The donkey couldn't remember when he completely forgot about the town. Was it the very night of the child's birth? Or sometime during the days when he fell in love with the gentleness of the shepherds? Daily they brought gifts of milk, butter, cheese and bread for the little family. He only knew he had never felt such contentment. For the first time in his whole life, he was glad he wasn't a camel. A poor couple would never have been able to hire a camel. He had to laugh at the thought. It was in the exact same moment that wisdom filled his heart, that voices called from outside the cave. The donkey thought he must be dreaming. Outside the cave stood royal guests. There were Persian carpet tents and camels, elephants, horses and beautiful animals the donkey had never before seen. Dressed in the finest splendor one could imagine were three Magi. They were offering gifts to the little barefoot child. These kings, who the donkey once dreamed of only passing by, were bowing to the mother of the child the donkey had himself carried and helped to make warm. No one saw the donkey in the cave as he knelt down and large tears fell from his eyes. He thought how close he had come to missing the real king. He thought how his own longing to be with the rich important men had robbed him of loving himself and who he was. And try as he might, he couldn't remember what he had seen so inviting in the noisy, busy town. Especially when the little boy was stroking his nose so gently.

One night, the family left Bethlehem. The little donkey wondered if he would ever see them again. He never stopped thinking of the little boy.

Many years passed, thirty and some, he guessed. The donkey found himself in Jerusalem during the time of a great feast. Everyone was talking of a great king who was coming to the city. The little donkey listened while his friends dreamed of someday carrying someone as important as a king. The donkey was thinking of a census long ago. Suddenly a man came and untied the little donkey. They heard the man saying something about the Master saying it was okay. The Master was going to ride a donkey into the city for the Passover celebration. The other donkeys whispered to him. Such is our lot in life. We have seen the Master in Jerusalem before. He is kind, but a poor man who wears sandals and is himself the friend of all the poor. Of course he would ride a donkey into the city, he is one of us. At least, they continued, nothing can stop us from catching a glimpse of the real king as he rides by. That will be enough.

The little donkey said nothing. He walked on the cobblestones. When he turned the corner he beheld the Master. In all the noise and rush of the crowd, the Master quietly stroked the donkey's nose. Tears slid down the donkey's face as he recognized the touch of the little boy he had dreamed of every night. He carried the Master as proudly as he could through the city. He walked right past his friends. But they never saw him. They had their heads turned to watch for the great horse and the splendid clothes that would tell them when the king was coming by. . . .

Love One Another As I Have Loved You

THEY SAT AT THE KITCHEN TABLE. HER YOUNG FACE, HER blue eyes were a mirror to her mother's. The kitchen window was open. The faded curtains were moving in the gentle breeze. With six children and eight grandchildren in the family, it was a rare moment indeed for the two of them to be alone. The mother took a sip from her coffee cup. "Something happened a while ago that made me very proud," she said. "My oldest sister and my youngest brother had a serious argument. Everyone in the family took their turn trying to reason with them. I decided to go and talk to my brother."

"As soon as he saw me, he knew why I had come. He said he was sorry, but nothing was going to change his mind. He wasn't going to forgive his sister. She was wrong and until she apologized, he wasn't ever going to speak to her again. I know how stubborn they both could be. I took his hand in mine and asked him if he remembered Ma. How the only thing she had ever asked was that we get along together. I told him, Ma and Pa are in heaven and they're looking down on us and watching us right this moment." The mother's eyes filled with tears and she could hardly finish the rest of it.

"My brother started crying," she said. "He remembered Ma, how her blue eyes would look right through us, and she would tell us that the only thing she wanted in this whole world was peace in her family. My brother said he would forgive his sister, not because he wanted to, but because Ma had asked him to. I was so proud that I was the one who changed his mind," she said.

They were both wiping their eyes when the door opened and one of her own brothers came in with his two children. Their mother quickly got up and started another pot of coffee. The daughter watched her. This gentle woman who worked endlessly for her children. She was there for all of them time and time again; babysitting, comforting, listening, encouraging, cooking, mending their wounds. While the world insisted that they grow up, she still saw them as her children, and it felt good. For all that, she asked only one thing in return, the same thing as her own mother, that they get along with one another. A small request for such love.

Despite their best intentions, they had their share of arguments. Each brother and sister was so different. Sometimes it was hard to believe they all came from the same parents. It was only because of their mother that there was still peace in the family.

The daughter thought of the story her mother had shared with her. It was especially sad because she knew her mother wanted that to be her own living memory, a memory that would continue to keep peace in her family even when she was no longer physically present with them.

It wasn't until the daughter lay in bed that night that the real meaning of all that had happened that day came to her. Love one another as I have loved you. The words washed over her like a wave that had been traveling from the sea and had finally reached the shore.

She had heard those words so often, yet had never actually seen them in terms of a real family. Was Jesus so alive to her, did she love him that much that she could forgive her brothers and sisters for Him? Simply because He was in heaven watching His children right this moment? Jesus. Loving all of His children, as different as they are. Laying down His life for each of them and asking only one thing in return. Love one another as I have loved you.

"Father, forgive them; they know not what they do."

IT WOULD BE SIMPLE TO LOOK AT THE PURSE AND THE thirty silver pieces and think Judas. Or to read the words, "Father, forgive them; they know not what they do," and think of the soldiers who crucified Him. It would be simple to do this, and for most of us, it is.

We must realize that the Bible is as alive today as it was when it was written some two thousand years ago. The Bible is our story. Every person has to believe that we are betraying Jesus when we turn our backs on the hungry, the poor, the homeless, or any of God's children.

At least the soldiers didn't know Him.

If we all truly believed His words, "Whatever we do for the least of our brothers, we do for Him," how could hunger continue to exist in a world that has more than enough food to provide for all of His children?

Perhaps one day all people will realize the Bible was written for us today, and live accordingly. Until that day arrives we, the believers, must lead the way for the rest of the world. We who know Jesus, who have shared His body and blood. We must live every day as if Jesus walked among us. For surely He does. He is the hungry, the poor, the homeless.

When the final day comes, when we meet Jesus, we do not want to be holding "the bag of silver."

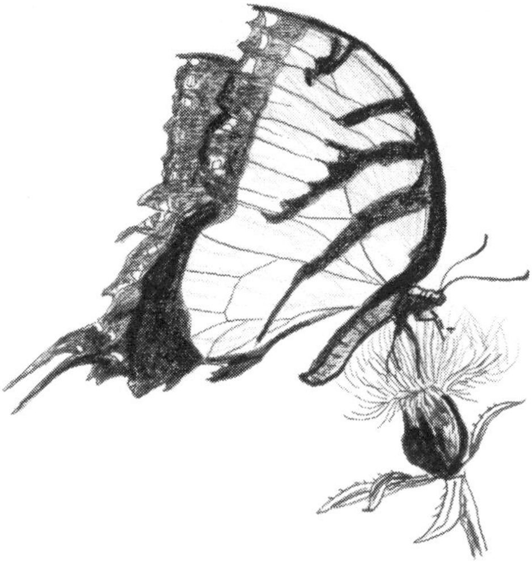

Pick Up Your Mat and Be Healed!

I SENT THE CHILDREN AND MY HUSBAND OFF TO MASS WITHout me. I stayed in bed, feeling quite sick and miserable. It seemed a long time before I heard the car drive into the driveway. My daughter ran up the steps and quietly peeked in my room. "Are you still sick?" she asked. "Yes," I answered. "I don't think I'll be getting up today."

She disappeared from my room in a flash. Two minutes later she was back, sitting on the side of my bed. "I have a story to read to you," she said. "And I want you to listen very closely to every word." She began to read in her most serious voice.

"One day Jesus was teaching, and the power of the Lord made him heal. Sitting close by were teachers of the law who had come from every village of Galilee and from Judea and Jerusalem." She slowly sounded out the long words. "Some men came along carrying a paralytic on a mat. They were trying to bring him in and lay him before Jesus, but they found no way of getting him through because of the crowd, so they went up on the roof. There they let him down with his mat through the tiles into the middle of the crowd before Jesus. He then said to the paralyzed man: "I say to you, stand up! Pick up your mat and go home." The man stood and picked up the mat he had been lying on and went home praising God.

She closed the Bible and looked right into my eyes. "Father read that story to us in church this morning," she said. "If you really believe, Jesus can heal you too." She then stood up, shook her finger at me, and said, "now pick up your mat and be healed!" She looked at me with such belief in her face that I had to get up no matter how sick I was feeling. But the strangest thing happened. A feeling of warmth slowly spread inside of me and it felt as soothing as a hot water bottle being placed directly on the pain. I got dressed. My daughter was overjoyed. "I knew you could do it!" she cried. "You just had to believe!"

Let the Children Come to Me

MY DAUGHTER LOVED TO READ THE BIBLE. WE THOUGHT it very touching. She was only seven, but ever since we decided to go to Bible study before Mass on Sunday, she often took out her jean Bible and read it aloud at home. One day, during lent, she took her Bible to my mother's house. How very proud she was that she could read it to us. Watching her filled me with a special joy, until my brother commented, "she doesn't even know what she's reading. Does she understand what the word repentance means? Listen to her. She's just repeating words." It's strange how quickly good air can be let out of a balloon.

Easter was the following Sunday. We were invited to my mother's house for dinner. She always had Easter baskets for my two children, her only grandchildren so far. It was our own family's tradition to attend the Easter Vigil on Saturday evening. My children loved to see the church in darkness. They got to hold a candle and watch the whole church fill up with light. Then on Sunday morning we didn't have to rush as much. Saturday night for God, I thought, and Sunday morning for the Easter bunny.

As always, my mother's ham dinner was superb. There is no better cook than she. We were all so busy enjoying the meal that we didn't notice my daughter had gone outside a while ago. The back of my mother's house is beautiful and safe. It's filled with pine trees and a stone wall that marks the edge of the property. Suddenly my daughter burst inside the house. She was excited and grabbed her Pepe's hand. "I have a surprise," she exclaimed. "You all have to come outside with me right now." Pepe got up immediately. It's amazing to see how quickly our parents respond to their grandchildren's requests. "Everybody up," my father said. "Let's see what my little pumpkin has planned for us."

She led us to the backyard. There were seven pine logs set up as seats. Each one had a pine branch placed on it. In the middle was another pine log with a jean Bible set on it. She directed all of us to our seats and told us the pine branches were for us to hold. When we were all seated she picked up her Bible and said, "I am going to read the 96th Psalm because this is Jesus' special day and I think He would want us to read to Him. I know it will make Him happy."

We listened to her read the words:

> Be glad, earth and sky!
>   Roar, sea, and all the creatures in you;
>   be glad, fields, and everything in you!
> Then the trees in the woods will
>   shout for joy before the Lord,
>   because he comes to rule the earth.
> He will rule all peoples of the world with
>   justice and fairness.

There she stood in her white first communion dress that was gently blowing in the breeze. Her little face was radiant, looking like a small and fragile flower standing in the woods under that enormous expanse of sky. No, she didn't understand what all the words meant. But she taught me something special that Easter. Maybe it isn't words that Jesus wants from us!

I Hate Having You To Come Home To

IT WAS A PERFECT SUMMER EVENING. YOU KNOW THE KIND. The temperature is just perfect. There's a slight breeze in the air, and you feel like you have control of your children for one more day.

Our son was sixteen then, and he asked if we felt like having some ice cream. Whenever your teenager wants to be with you, you take advantage of it. So we were off, riding to our favorite ice cream place. And out of the silence, our son said, "I hate having you to come home to." He was never one to waste words.

"Could you tell us what you mean by that?," I asked, "You hate having us to come home to." He looked at us and said. "You know, my friends can do anything they want to do. They don't have a curfew. They come home drunk. As a matter of fact, one of my friend's parents thinks it's funny when he comes home drunk. But you and dad are so serious about everything. It's really hard for me to do what

I want to do. You know the kind of relationship we have, and that's what makes it hard." He looked at us, trying to understand all of it. "Why does everything I do have to affect you?" he asked.

My husband asked him some questions. "What do you want us to tell you, go ahead and drink all you want? Come home anytime you feel like it, we don't care? Things are either right or wrong. And as your parents we can never tell you to do what is wrong."

I asked him, "Isn't the relationship we have worth the small price of following our rules? Isn't the love we share worth it? Everything we have is yours. We live our life for you. Each single thing we do we do for our family. That isn't enough?"

But I don't think he was too sure. He answered quite weakly, "Yeah, I guess so."

When I got home, I really wanted to understand his side of it. It was obviously a struggle. I remember praying to understand the way he was feeling. Then God showed me. I didn't like the vision I saw. I didn't like how well I suddenly understood. The thought was clear, the message unmistakeable. Sometimes I hate the relationship I have with Jesus. Sometimes I hate having Him to come home to, especially when someone's mean to me or someone hurts me. I think, oh, I could be so much meaner than they. I know just how I could do it. Just what I could say to cut them down. And how I'd love to be selfish sometimes, just to do what I want to do. I hate having to consider the poor all the time. I hate knowing that what I do affects their lives. Sometimes it's hard knowing the kind of relationship I have with Jesus. And I thought again about children and how they know your rules. They know what you want them to do. Yet, they'll say, "I didn't know you meant that." Yet, how often I do that with Jesus. "Oh, I didn't know you meant that." Forgive my enemies. Love those who hate me. He couldn't have meant that. He doesn't know what those people did.

But he does mean that, and that's the kind of relationship, that love relationship, that I have with him.

It was strange to look at myself as Jesus' teenager. Coming home to him as my parent. It made me aware of the kind of struggle a teenager goes through. The love is there, and you want to make them happy, yet you want to do what you want to do. Isn't following the rules a small price to pay for the love we share? I thought again.

Yet, the rules get broken. You pull away despite the great love. But how wonderful the feeling is when you return. He is always waiting, always willing to take you back and love you unconditionally. Tonight, in the sacrament of reconciliation, I feel the miracle of having someone like Jesus to come home to.

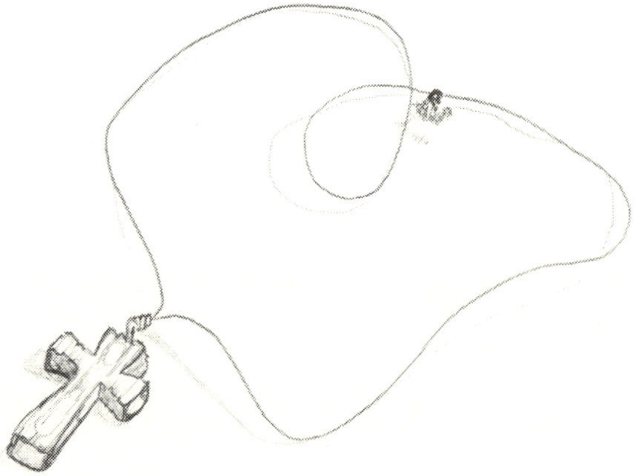

So, What's Church Like These Days?

SHE SAT IN THE WAITING ROOM. AS FAR AS SHE COULD tell there were three lab technicians on duty. She didn't try to figure out who could take blood the best. She would get who she was meant to.

Suddenly a tall, slim, young man in his late twenties appeared from a back room and motioned to her to follow him. He led her to what looked like an old-fashioned school desk. "Wait here," he said, "I'll be right back."

She could hear him talking to the other lab technician behind the white curtain that separated the rooms. "What good is a two week vacation when they won't give you the time off to take it?" he complained. "These sixty hour weeks are killing me. I don't need the overtime. I need St. Thomas or The Islands. Just get me out of this place."

"Haven't even been able to get to the old condo on weekends lately, have you?" a pleasant voice teased. "Now that's what I call a rough life. Why don't you tie the knot like the rest of us? That would solve your travel problems." "Seriously," she continued, "you've got a great girlfriend. What are you waiting for?"

"I don't know what I want," he replied. "I guess I'm bored with the whole thing."

He came back into the room where she was waiting. He pulled up a chair opposite her and quickly scanned her chart. He looked directly into her eyes and said, "I'm going to cut you to see how good you bleed. Is that all right with you?"

She could see he was trying to get a rise out of her. She steadily met his gaze, held out her arm and replied, "sounds good to me, cut away."

He seemed amused at the calmness of her reply. He took out something that looked like a rubber band. In one second he had gently slashed a cut on her upper arm. As the blood prickled out, he soaked it up with a white blotter.

"We'll be here for a while," he said very matter-of-factly. "This is a new test they do to see how fast your blood clots. That gives the doctor an indication if you'll need blood during the operation." "Don't worry," he said, "you clot good." She smiled. They were quiet for a moment.

"Why do you wear a cross?" he asked unexpectedly, as he suddenly noticed the simple brown wooden cross that hung on a black rope around her neck. "Are you some kind of religious?"

"No," she laughed. "I guess you could say this is my church cross. Many of us wear it as a sign of our church community. I wear it more for myself than anyone else. It reminds me of something I once read that we should treat every person as if Jesus stood between us."

"So, what's church like these days?" he asked. "I used to go to church every Sunday when I was a kid. Even was an altar boy, the whole bit. I don't even remember exactly when or why I stopped going. I figure there's really nothing there for someone like me who is still single and has no children."

"You'd be surprised to know there's a lot going on for people like you." "At our church we have several small Bible groups that meet weekly. It's really more a sharing of where your life is at, even though it is based on Scripture reading. It's quite interesting and many single people are part of it. It seems to have made quite a difference in their lives. There's a lot of things you could do. A lot of things you could be involved in. It's obvious you've been blessed with a great many gifts and talents. You have a lot to share in community. But you'll never know what plan Jesus has for your life unless you go back. Jesus really does talk to you in the Word, when you're ready and open to listen. Why not try it one more time?"

He seemed very interested. He rubbed his chin. "You know," he said, "I just might do that."

By this time the blood had stopped. He got up from his chair. "Good luck with the operation," he said. "You'll do just fine. They see cases like yours every day. They know just what to do."

"And good luck with church," she said, wishing she could tell him the same.

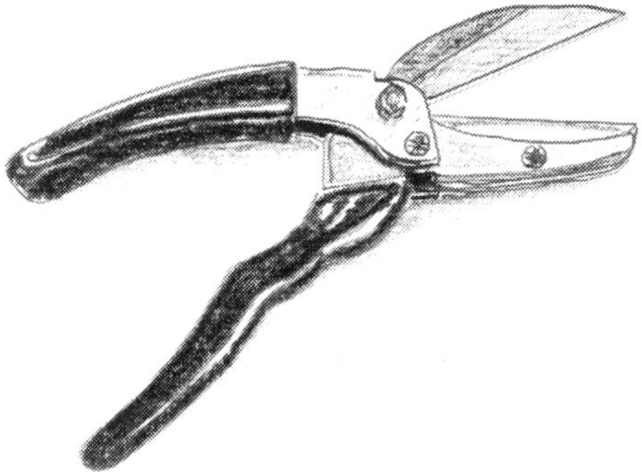

Pruning

THEY DIDN'T WANT TO GO. WHAT WAS ALL THIS TALK about devil worship and backmasking anyway? Every generation had its music. No parents liked it. What was the big deal with today's music?

Their two teenage children did not want to go either. Yet, the four of them were in the church hall when the meeting began. There were more teenagers there than parents. Most of them wore rock tee shirts and ripped jeans.

The young man who directed the program began by explaining the symbols on the album covers. As he played some of the songs, many parents were shocked indeed to hear the words their thirteen-year-olds were singing. Words being sung in their own homes, but never really registering. There were quite a few red faces in the audience, and all of them were over thirty. Some of the stories of how the songs were written were quite frightening, as was the backmasking itself. The meeting lasted an hour. The home discussion lasted late into the night. The feeling of communicating as a family was a good one. Much understanding surfaced that evening. Each person was left to make their final decision on the matter.

A week later, the daughter was sitting on the couch when it suddenly occured to her mother that she hadn't heard her play her tapes for some time. Tapes that were her favorite and played every minute on the hour. "What happened to those tapes you play over and over again?" her mother asked. "I threw them away" her daughter answered. "I can't bring myself to listen to a person who wears a cross in that way and says the things she says about Jesus." "I couldn't believe it myself," her mother said. "Don't you think that everyone who was at the meeting will have to throw their tapes away too?" The daughter shook her head thoughtfully. "Not everyone has the kind of relationship with Jesus that we do," she answered. "A tree will be known by the fruit that it bears," her mother said.

She studied her young daughter. How quickly she was growing, and not so unlike a young fruit tree. Planting is the easy part. The hard part is in the pruning. What branches will be sacrificed to make the trunk grow strong? Human nature whispers, keep them all, you might need them. See how full they make the tree look. But in your heart you understand that some of the branches must be cut to return the energy to the source of life. Only then will the tree be strong enough to bear fruit.

It happily occurred to the mother that she had experienced her daughter's difficult decision to prune her life for Jesus.

The Mother's Curse

"MOM, I WANT TO ASK YOU SOMETHING AND I WANT YOU to promise you won't get mad" he said. "I promise," she answered. "Just say, now I'm not saying I want to do this, but just say I tell you that I don't want to go to church anymore. Will you make me go?"

The question took her by surprise. She pictured herself at his age, just turning fifteen. That was the year she swore to her mother that she would never make her children go to church if they didn't want to. She was sure this was part of the curse her mother had placed on her.

"Let me think about it," she told her son. "I'll let you know when I've made my decision." She knew her children were too smart for quick answers. And, "Because I said so" had stopped working long ago.

It was three days before she decided what to tell him. She called him in the living room. "I have a question to ask you," she began. "If I told you that starting tomorrow you didn't have to go to school anymore, would you go?"

"Of course not," he answered. "But you love school," she said. "You know you'd miss your friends. You'd be bored all alone at home. And you wouldn't be able to go to college like you've always planned. Knowing that, why wouldn't you keep going to school?"

"Because I'm a kid," he answered. "And if you give a kid a choice to stay home from school, he will." As soon as the words were out, he realized the point his mother was making.

"Let me tell you something," she said. "Even as a parent I don't have the final say if you'll go to school or not. Somewhere along the line people felt that an education was so necessary to make it in life, that they passed a law saying that all children have a right to one. Well, as your mother, I feel there is something even more important for you to make it in this world. And that is Jesus."

"If you became the president of a billion-dollar corporation and left Jesus out of your life, you would not be successful in my eyes. But if you keep Jesus in your life, no matter what you do, you will be a success. Right now you probably feel I am taking away your choice about church. But it doesn't work that way. I remember asking my brother one day why he never went on to play professional tennis. He was the best in the high school and had unbelievable endurance and ability. He told me that wasn't enough. It's the kids who have a tennis racket put in their hands when they're five or six who have a choice to go on to play professional tennis. At fifteen, it's already too late."

"I look at it this way. For eighteen years they make you stay in school. That gives you the choice of whether or not you will go on to college. You couldn't make that choice unless someone forced you to go to school. Same thing happens with piano lessons, sports, dance, etc."

"You don't have a choice unless you've had the lessons. Church is no different. For eighteen years, I will keep God in your life so you can have a chance to know Him. At eighteen you will have to make the choice if church is something you want to keep. My job as your mother is giving you the opportunity to make that choice. Do you see that?"

He seemed satisfied with the answer. "Well," he said, "I just thought I'd ask." He turned to go back up to his room.

She thought of the hard times she had given her own mother. Oh, how many times she had said, "I'll never do that to my kids." How different life looks from the other side of the fence. She smiled. I guess it's all part of the mother's curse.

The Fourth Pile

IT WAS GOING TO BE THAT KIND OF A DAY, SHE COULD tell already. The sky was a perfect blue. The air was crisp and clean charging everything with a burst of energy. Dreams were just a matter of making them come true. Life was so simple and clear on a day like this that she wondered how she could slip so far away from that feeling.

"Ma, are those cinnamon rolls I smell?" called a sleepy voice from upstairs. "You bet they are, and they'll be ready in five minutes. Wake your sister and come downstairs. I have something special planned for today."

Between bites, Trevor asked, "What is it? Is it a surprise?" "Kind of," she answered. "Thanksgiving is next week. The whole family is going to Nana's house for dinner. Your three cousins, Emily, Jillian and Alanna will be there. I thought you might want to go through our bookcase and give them all the little children's books we've finished reading." "Okay," Trevor said. "We'll separate the books into three piles, one for Em, one for Jill, and one for Alanna." "Oh, won't that be a great surprise?" Jessie said.

They couldn't wait to begin. They went to the bookcase and Trevor handed Jessie the little children's books. She brought the piles of them to the braided rug. When the books were all there, they sat cross-legged on the floor and began the sorting.

"Who do you think would like this one?" Trevor asked, holding up a book with a squirrel on the cover. "Jillian," Jessie answered without hesitation. The book went into Jillian's pile.

She watched for a while, amazed at how well they knew their little cousins. Jillian was definitely the animal lover. All the girls, even at the tender age of two and a half, had their own likes and dislikes. It was touching to see how very serious Trevor and Jessie were in making sure each book was perfect for each cousin.

She was cleaning; vacuuming and polishing. But she kept being drawn to the piles growing on the rug and an inner wish she couldn't suppress to have the three of them all squeeze again into that big over-stuffed rocker. Before she knew it, the cuckoo clock rang eleven times. How could time fly by so quickly, she wondered.

"We're finished, Ma," they called out. They pointed proudly to the piles. "This one's for Emily, this one's for Jillian, and this one's for Alanna." "You did a wonderful job," she praised, looking at the neat piles on the rug. At the same time her eyes caught another pile of books partly hidden behind Trevor. "Did you forget those?" she asked, pointing to that pile.

"Well," he said shyly. "If it's all right with you we thought we'd keep these. "Of course," she answered. "You can keep any ones you want."

That settled, they jumped up, quite satisfied with what they had decided. "You go out and play for awhile and I'll call you when it's time for lunch," she said. "I'm very proud of both of you. This will be a great Thanksgiving surprise."

As they ran out the door, she sat on the braided rug, curious about this fourth pile. She was surprised to see that on the very top of the pile was her favorite little book. She laughed aloud. Those little rascals! All those years she thought she was so clever reading that book to them over and over. The book she loved about a family who always helped one another. She thought using that book was her idea. Now she could see that this little book was their secret weapon. They knew that anytime they wanted her to read, they had only to get this book and she could never resist the chance to read the story again.

The second book in the pile was one they could all recite word for word. It was the book that had taught them little a and big A; the pages were worn with learning. Quickly she looked at the rest of the books in the pile. Slowly she realized the books in the fourth pile were the story of their lives, a story that had been written in the arms of that overstuffed rocker. It was something that could never be given away.

She walked over to the bookcase. She still read to them. Now the books looked different as she wondered which new ones would make it to the fourth pile. Her eyes scanned the titles of the books and stopped to rest on one book that stood unopened on the second shelf. She smiled, picked it up and planned a story from it for that very night. Feeling a new peace she had never before experienced, she walked to the screen door to call the children in for lunch. The book lay on the rug, the sun streaming in the window catching on the gold lettering on the cover that read—The Bible.

The Bushel Basket

"GERRY, WE'RE HOME," I SAID, GENTLY SHAKING MY youngest brother's shoulder to wake him. "Was everything okay?" I asked.

He rolled off the couch rubbing his eyes while mumbling in his sleep, "they asked me to bless them."

"What?" I asked, not sure I had heard right.

"After they climbed into bed, they asked me to bless them."

"And did you?" I asked.

"Yes," he answered.

He turned and stumbled down the hallway still half asleep. I knew my little brother enough to know that was the end of the conversation. "Gerry, thanks for babysitting tonight. We'll see you at Ma's tomorrow, okay? Brian will give you a ride home."

I watched him walk down the stairs and stood in the doorway until the car was out of sight. In the night's stillness I thought about my little brother, his famous football huddles, all the kids in the neighborhood gathered at our house; the mystery always being the second Gerry arrived, so did all of them.

There were giant baseball games and basketball games, and it truly surprised me to watch his gentleness with the kids. Jessie, my daughter, was always on his team. The little scrapper, he called her. And believe me, in her eagerness to please him she often surprised him with her ability. Thinking of what kind of role model Gerry was, it was even that much harder for me to picture the kids, Trevor especially, asking Gerry to bless them. And the more I thought about it, the more I couldn't wait to ask Trevor and Jessie about it in the morning.

"Did Gerry say anything more about blessing the kids?" I asked my husband Brian as he walked in the front door.

"You know Gerry," he answered. "He was asleep the whole way home."

"You know, I didn't even think of it before now, but this is the first night we haven't put the kids to bed ourselves since we started the beautiful tradition Father explained of blessing the children each night before they go to bed. Isn't it nice to know it's become so much a part of their bedtime that they'd ask Gerry to bless them? Somehow I can't picture my fifteen-year-old brother blessing the kids," I said. "Neither can I," my husband replied as we shut out the lights.

For once, I didn't mind that Trevor and Jessie were up early.

"Well, did you two have fun with Gerry last night?" I began.

"Yeah," they both answered. "Gerry taught us a new basketball game and we played till dark. Then he made popcorn and, you won't get mad, will you, but he let us stay up way past our bedtime."

"Did Gerry tuck you in and put you to bed?" I asked.

"Yes," they answered.

"Did you ask Gerry to bless you?" I asked.

"Yes, and you know what?" they both said in complete surprise. "He didn't even know how! So we told him what you do. Just make a little sign of the cross on our forehead and say, I bless you in the Name of the Father, the Son and the Holy Spirit."

"And did he?" I asked.

"Well," they both grinned, "he picked up our light saber and blessed us both with that, but he said the words right."

"Come here, both of you. Come sit beside me on the bed. Do you know what you did last night?"

"No," they answered.

"Well," I said, "last night you took the light from under the bushel basket and hung it for all the world to see. Jesus told us that no one lights a lamp and then hides it or puts it under a basket; instead, he puts it on the lampstand, so that people may see the light as they come in. You both know that the real light is Jesus, and you could have put Him under the basket so Gerry wouldn't have seen Him. But you decided not to." They listened wide-eyed. "You weren't embarrassed or afraid to tell Gerry that Jesus was your friend and each night when you go to bed you want His blessing. And do you know the only thing Gerry mentioned when we came home last night? Well, it wasn't about the basketball game or the popcorn or even that you stayed up late. The only thing he said was that you asked him to bless you. And when he got home, Nana said he told her and Pepe about it. And Nana and Pepe told my sisters and brothers. And each time the story was told, there was the face of Jesus, like a bright light, placed on the lampstand for everyone to see. All because of the two of you."

"And know what else? When Gerry has a little boy or a little girl of his own, he'll remember the night you taught him how to bless you. And I'll bet he won't even need to use a light saber!"

Brother Red

THERE WAS NO ONE MORE STUBBORN THAN HE, NOR MORE gentle. Simply said, he was a man from the old school. What she loved most about him was that they never had to talk about the weather. They plunged right into the very heart of religion or politics, mostly religion. The conversation always began with a major issue, for instance, do we have the right to kill? As the night waned on, the world became smaller until they ended the discussion with their usual dialogue. "So, what's wrong with owning a new car?" she'd ask. "As long as you give your fair share to the poor."

"I don't deserve it," he'd reply, with that winsome grin of his. "How can I deserve to buy a new car when 'my brother' down the road has no place to sleep tonight?" Quickly, he'd spread his giant hands open in a gesture of nonreproach and continue. "Now, I'm not trying to say you or anybody else shouldn't own one. I'm just saying I don't feel right buying one."

"You put yourself on a guilt trip," she replied. "You're too good a man for that. You do more for the poor than anyone I know."

"I'm set in my ways," he'd say. "Maybe it's this red hair that makes me so stubborn." Then he'd search her face and bare his soul. "The whole truth is, one day I'll have to answer to the man upstairs for every decision I make. And I just haven't figured out yet how I'd justify owning a new car."

How she loved this man!

Brother Red died suddenly in the spring, so quickly, so young. Many wonderful things were said at his funeral. How he gave so generously to the poor, not only with money but with his time. There were so many heartwarming stories told about this man who was husband, father, banjo player, singer, co-worker, church member and friend to all.

But to her, his automobile, as he called it, was a symbol of all he stood for. This simple man who refused the luxury of owning a new car when his 'brother' had no place to sleep.

This very day, she thought, he was answering for the decisions he made in his life. And now, he was getting what he truly deserved.

It was no coincidence to her that his automobile was in the garage being repaired the day he died.

Sometimes the Eyes Can't See

THEY STOOD THERE WITH EAGER FACES. THEIR EYES WERE smiling and they were ready. It was a surprise to all of us that a passing thought had become a reality, and we really couldn't believe we were standing outside our own little garden gate. That was the beginning.

Seven years ago there was a discussion of ways our church could share its wealth with its people. The first thing that popped into my mind was all the land most churches own, including our own. Without thinking I blurted out, "Why doesn't the church sponsor a community garden? We use up so much of our land in manicured lawns when it could be producing food for many of our families." To my surprise, Father immediately took me up on my suggestion. He asked me if I was a garden person myself. When I said yes, he asked me to think about planning a community garden in the spring. It seemed so safe then to say yes. The snow blanketed the ground and spring seemed years away. Months passed and I was almost relieved that no more was mentioned about it. It occured to me what a large project this was. What if I failed?

But Father did remember. In March he called to tell me of a plot of land near the rectory that belonged to the church. Could we use that for the community garden? The sound of his voice was so gentle, so hopeful, that I forgot about failing and just said yes. At that moment I was determined to have the best community garden anyone had ever seen. Visions of thirty "Crockett" gardens in a row filled my eyes. I couldn't wait to get started.

The initial preparation was hard. The abandoned field was strewn with litter. It had been neglected for years. A group of faithful friends and neighbors of the church land cleaned the land. We hired a local farmer who patiently harrowed and spread manure and plowed until the land looked quite ready. My husband and a friend installed a six foot fence enclosing the garden on all sides. Next, we plotted our thirty gardens and set out to find thirty families to care for them. It was fun making posters and writing letters to promote our garden. My own family had found such closeness working in our home garden that it was quite easy for me to paint a picture of yesteryear when families worked together to make things grow. The signatures on our list grew steadily. Each week we chatted about the seeds we had ordered and how we had already planned our gardens. Then came the exciting day when our eager families gathered outside our fence.

The first year was a dream come true. Garden by garden was rototilled until the little field glistened in the sunshine. You entered our garden gate and a feeling of peace entered with you. Each garden spoke of its people and the only real chore became leaving it. People proudly painted garden signs announcing their gardens. Many families planted flowers as borders. On Sunday many of our church people would walk through the garden showing their own children how to grow beans, or what potatoes looked like. It was amazing how some of the children had no idea that potatoes grew in the ground. The garden was becoming quite a talk of the church. Many people planted gardens of their own at home such was the excitement our community garden generated. Oh, the taste of success was sweet.

By the third year there was a slight drop in interest. So we bought a picnic table and initiated monthly picnic/volleyball games to keep the spirit alive. We gathered happily under the giant oak tree and spread our blankets around her. We shared garden news, fun, and friendship. We had a harvest Mass in November. We decorated the church with corn stalks, pumpkins and old milk jugs. We shared in the memory of a joyful summer together.

But the fast pace of life took its toll. The garden began to look shabby. The fifth year the garden was filled with weeds. Despite people's best intentions, they were just too busy. I felt the garden was becoming a failure. What did people think now as they drove by on Sunday mornings? Perhaps we should just close it, I thought.

Soon after that thought I was standing in one corner of the garden looking despairingly at the growth. At the far end of the garden a father and his son had just arrived. Eagerly they brought over the garden hose. The father stood looking so peacefully, watering what looked to me like a small disaster. Their entire garden was overgrown. The spinach had bolted. The beans had popped open their sides in ugly bulges from being overripe. I walked over to say hi. He smiled and said. "You know, I had forgotten the feeling of a garden, the escape. This is the only place in my life where time has no meaning." His little boy looked up with sparkling eyes and proudly pointed to the sunflowers he and his dad had planted together. Every week they came faithfully to water them. And each week he stood measuring how tall they were next to him. They were quite content with their "harvest." Somehow they didn't seem to even notice the weeds.

The garden adjacent to theirs looked just as pitiful. This was quite a surprise. That had been one of the most cared for gardens of all. A few weeks later I ran into the woman who had planted that garden. With tear-filled eyes she told me how she and her father had planted that garden together. Her father had patiently and tenderly showed her how to plant beans and tomatoes and cukes. Then, without any warning, he died of a sudden heart attack. That garden would be an everlasting memory of the last precious summer she had spent with him.

The land was planting its own seed in each of us. The seed sprouted in different ways, giving to each family the harvest they needed. For some, the land gave beautiful vegetables. For others, it gave quiet time to be together. It was a time for making memories. And for all of us, it sowed a bond of friendship that grew like the mighty asparagus, returning year after year because of its deep roots.

I love to walk through the garden. Each garden speaks of the many families who cared for it. I realize that only the land really knows their story. It amazes me how differently the garden looks to me now. Oh, I still see the weeds. But now I can look beyond them. The garden has taught me some wonderful things about growth. The important thing is to plant the seed. It is not our task to worry about what grows from it. God will see to that.

Our church is warm and alive. As a mother, a wife and an active member of our parish, I want to be part of many more plantings. I feel the garden has taught me the lessons I need to continue. Don't be afraid to risk. Do what you believe in. Don't look for success in yourself or others, for there is so much the eyes can't see!

What Would Jesus Say?

THEY WERE SITTING IN A BIG CIRCLE, MOSTLY MOTHERS. Their children were preparing for their first Penance. They were upstairs in the church, the parents were in the church basement. They were talking about sin, about their own first confessions, about Catholic schools and clappers. One parent was saying that her children's fighting was on the top of her list. She was at her wit's end. She wondered if any other mothers had this problem. She explained to her children, often, about being good. Yet, they continued to argue and fight day in and day out.

There was one woman in the group who had older children. She laughed and said, "One day my two children were really going at it. I know just how you feel. I had had it. I separated them and asked my son, what would Jesus say if He could see you now? My son looked at me, not the least bit shaken, and answered that Jesus would probably say, now there's two normal kids. We talked about being good. He told me he didn't think that fighting with his sister was a sin. That was how they played. 'What do you expect me to do?' he asked. 'Come home from school and say, sister, dear, I missed you?' Of course, 'Hi, puke,' was a far cry from that. He said I should be worried if they refused to have anything to do with one another. My son then told me he was worried, worried about me. Can you imagine? He said I took life too seriously. That I should lighten up. 'You must know that we really love each other,' he said. "It's just not normal to go around saying it. And I won't be telling you I love her again,' he concluded.

I thought a lot about that conversation. Many times I confuse human behavior in a family with sin. Sibling rivalry is a way for our children to learn how to solve their problems. It teaches them how to deal with conflict in the outside world. They can only work those things out in an atmosphere of unconditional love. That's part of what families are for. Of course, it's not always so easy while it's happening.

My two children are the best of friends. They still argue, wrestle, and call each other names. But their relationship is a beautiful one. When my son returned home from college, it was obvious he missed all of us. But long after our lights had been shut off, I could hear their voices whispering of dreams and plans and secrets. I pictured the two of them and knew exactly what Jesus would say.

A Knock at the Door

WHEN MY DAUGHTER WAS LITTLE SHE HAD GREAT DIFFI-culty learning to tell time. That was, of course, in the predigital days. My husband devoted a lot of time drawing clock faces and patiently teaching her until he thought she had mastered it. Well, a few weeks later he wanted to know what time it was, so he asked her to run and look for him. After some hesitation a little voice softly called, "the big hand's on the 8 and the little hand's on the 3." "Jess," he said in disbelief, "you still don't know how to tell time, do you?" "No," she confessed. "Well," he asked, "just when do you think you're going to learn?" To his surprise, she looked not the least bit worried about the whole thing. And she answered very matter-of-factly, "Someday I'll just know."

After all, didn't her older brother know how to tell time? No one ever showed him. So she figured when you reach a certain age you just know about things.

I found her logic quite amusing until I was honest enough to admit how that same someday exists in my own life. As a matter of fact, twelve years ago the Bible was on the top of my "someday I'll just know" list. Oh, I wanted to read the Bible and tried to many times. I never knew just where or how to begin. I would usually begin with the New Testament. Then I would feel that I was in the middle of a story. So I'd go back to the Old Testament and soon find myself very confused. The solution was to shut the Bible and put it away for another year. But as long as I kept it on the someday shelf, I felt safe. Well, I probably would still be saying that if something very traumatic had not happened to change all that.

It happened when my husband's younger sister moved to California. She was my best friend. We grew up together and she was my roommate when I went to college. She was the one who was there during the questioning time of my faith. Now let me tell you that a more fanatic, letter-of-the-law Catholic never existed. And I could never even get her to question limbo, never mind admit that eating a hot dog on Friday had to be a greater sacrifice than having a clam plate and onion rings. And I think how often I tried to get her to question, not give up, just question her faith. So when I received her letter from California, it was more than a shock. She wrote that this very nice woman had gone to her home and asked her if she could read the Bible with her. She saw no harm in that. In fact, she always wanted to read the Bible. So she began to study weekly with this woman. The woman advised her not to tell her family that she was studying with her because they might not understand. Now five years later she had written to tell me she was being baptized into the Jehovah's Witnesses. She couldn't wait to see me, because now she had all the answers to any questions I might have. She moved back to Vermont a year later. Looking back now, I realize the move was for one purpose only—to save her mother and father, her two brothers and me. For only Jehovah's Witnesses will survive Armaggedon and come back to inherit the new earth. This is the basis of their beliefs. Naturally, she wanted her family to be there to inherit the earth with her.

Do you know what the hardest part was when she came back? It was constantly having to say, "I don't know." "No, I never read that." "It says what in Daniel?" And I thought

Daniel was about some lions in a den. After all those years of hearing about the Acts of the Apostles and Paul's letters to the Galatians, I had to admit I didn't really know who the Galatians were, never mind why Paul was writing letters to them and we were reading those letters during the liturgy on Sunday. And now, almost daily, I was with a person who in thirty seconds could turn a comment on the price of a quart of milk into a Bible discussion.

The Bible had suddenly come off the someday list. It had to be dealt with now. Not just for her, but for myself, my own questions. I was determined to learn the Bible once and for all.

A few of us at our church got together and pushed for our own Bible study. Twelve years ago a Bible sharing started on Sunday mornings before our Sunday liturgy. At first I went alone. I figured I would learn how to read the Bible and then I would teach it to my children. The truth is I was a little afraid that the children would ask me questions that I couldn't answer. Every week I'd come home from Bible sharing and tell my husband what we had discussed. But he had his own questions and wanted to come to Bible sharing too. So we talked about the whole family going. Our son was in the third grade and our daughter was in the second grade. At that level they were already working on an Apple computer and reading books we read in junior high. Our son could name the whole hockey team and their goals for the season. It suddenly dawned on me that he couldn't name the twelve Apostles. Just when would my children learn the Bible? And for the first time an absolutely frightening thought entered my mind. When they were ready, who would be their teacher? Suddenly the vision of a nice woman knocking on their door gave me a chill. At that moment I knew I wanted them to learn the Bible at our church. So we decided to come to Bible sharing as a family. It was hard. I had to give up a lot; like the bathroom for instance. And the quiet Sunday mornings that I previously slipped out on my own became a rush of four people trying to get ready. For the last four years a paper route was added. But of all the family decisions we have ever made, that was not only the best, but the one that would change our lives forever.

Perhaps at this point you are wondering if a family can read the Bible at home on their own. Maybe you can, I couldn't. To be perfectly honest, I don't have enough discipline to set an hour aside every week and do it without fail. Also, I had much too many questions myself, never mind teaching it to others. For us, it made more sense to be part of a Bible study and it really felt good to make the commitment. When I thought of the hours of piano lessons, of basketball practice, of everything else we ran around for, suddenly an hour a week for the Bible didn't seem like too much.

We told the children we would all be going to Bible sharing because we wanted to learn more about Jesus. Also, because I had a lot of questions I didn't want them to have when they got to be my age. Once they saw we were going every week, no questions asked, they accepted it just like they do going to school.

We have studied the Bible every week for twelve years now. At first I was looking for answers. I really thought that's how the Bible worked, and if I studied it long enough, like my friend, I too would know all the answers. It took years for me to realize the Bible is not an answer book. It is the story of the relationship between God and us, His people. It is not a history book, it is our story. Many times the Bible was confusing. Some weeks I left with questions, sometimes even doubt. And when we read Exodus I think I found out why. In Exodus Moses asks God why He didn't lead His people by the coast. Why had He taken them the long way through the desert. And God answered that He led them through the desert so that He would be sure they wanted to be His people. They couldn't find that out if they took the short cut. I guess that's the bottom line. There is no short cut to having a relationship with God.

We have worked hard to develop our relationship with God. The Bible is encased in a shell, and you have to break open the shell in order to get inside. The shell is the culture and symbols of Our Lord's time. One example being the most basic symbol of bread. It took on an entire new meaning as we learned what bread meant to the people of those times.

Part of the shell is understanding if the writers were writing history, poetry or apocolyptic writing. The more we understood the background, the culture and the symbols of the Bible, the closer we could come to understanding the true message of Jesus's words to us.

There is only one thing I place above my own closeness with the Lord. That is the peace of knowing my children have come to know Him in a way no one will ever take away. They have a solid background of the Bible.

Each day of our lives, we have the opportunity to teach our children the Scriptures. And if we fail to do so, perhaps they will learn His Word in a way we never intended—by a knock on the door.

"Who Do My Friends Say That I Am?"

"ANYONE WHO WOULD LIKE TO STAY AFTER MASS TO HELP plan for Pat's funeral arrangements is very welcome to do so," Father announced just before the closing blessing at the Sunday Liturgy.

So many stayed. Some sat in the benches, some stood near the door; no one knowing quite how to begin. Then a voice was heard above the others, "what will we do now? Pat was the one who always handled everything?" She smiled thoughtfully and went on to answer her own question. "Somehow," she said with a very determined voice, "I know Pat will lead us through this too." Everyone present felt the strength of those words and gathered in the front benches of our church to begin fitting the pieces together.

The wake would be held in church on Monday evening. Earth flowers from the woods and the fields would dress the altar. Yes, Pat would definitely want liturgical dancing; a perfect meditation. The farewell procession would be a walk to the cemetery followed by a reception in the church hall. Every step in Pat's farewell celebration was to be handled by her immediate family together with her church family. Everything kept simple. Everything embroidered with meaning and real beauty—the pattern of the life Pat had woven.

The day of the wake kept all hands busy, keeping tears at bay, and allowing each of us the comfort of true mourning. The church was open and families came in and out all day; visiting, checking if anyone needed help, bringing in wild flowers. "We just came back from the woods," one mother said, coming through the door with her hands full. "We picked these wild flowers for Pat," and she smiled to her teenaged son as she spoke. "I can't really explain it, but it was so peaceful gathering the flowers. We had a chance to talk together and be at rest. What a beautiful idea it was to have hand-picked flowers!"

Soon the entire altar, the small tables, the floor spaces were filled with these "peaceful moments"; each tiger lily, wild daisy, cattail, Queen Anne's Lace, Rose of Sharon, speaking of the hands that had taken such care to find them.

Little vases full of the free jewels of the earth graced each table downstairs waiting to complement the food friends were preparing with the same great love. Seven o'clock came quickly and we all gathered at the end of the church to welcome home our dearest friend Patricia.

We stood shoulder to shoulder, the presence of the Lord holding us, giving us strength, and at that moment it seemed so natural that Pat should be coming to us, as community, the way she had each day of her life.

There was a time for private visiting and farewells, and then the church sat in silence. Father turned and said, "Why don't we all share something about Pat—some way she came into our lives."

"I remember the night we did that banner," someone began, and they pointed to a banner hanging in church. "We didn't know how we were going to finish it, so we knocked on Pat's door and she cut out the letters and made them fit perfectly with what seemed so little effort."

"She was that kind of person," a man said. "She never seemed in a hurry, yet she had hundreds of projects going and finished each in its time. And you'd never know it, that's the amazing part, everything she did was so quiet and unassuming."

"I remember when we first started the family religious education program," another person added. "Everything was so vague and complex, and it was Pat who quietly sorted it all out and made sense of it as she was always able to do."

"When we first came to church here we didn't know anyone," a woman said. "And one Sunday morning Pat came and invited us to her house for breakfast and talk. That was the beginning of us really feeling a part of our church family."

"She called me one beautiful Saturday morning to tell me she was admitted to the hospital the night before," a woman said. "She just wanted me to know because she said I always prayed so hard for her. I asked to see her right away, but she said no. She wanted to picture me in my garden on a day like this. Pat always put you where she knew you wanted to be."

"Pat was the one who made the very first costumes for our liturgical dancers," someone remembered. "She always wanted new ways to pray."

The church was still for a time, each of us trying to come to grips with her death. Our prayers for her healing, prayed with such belief she would be healed, now turned to trust in the Lord. Knowing, in the end, it has to be His Will. It was good His presence was there at the wake, to comfort us and mourn with us.

The hardest part of the wake was leaving, for we suddenly realized we didn't come to say goodbye to Pat, but to share what we would always keep of her.

The folk group played the first song of the funeral Mass. Father stepped to the pulpit. "This is a robe Pat made for me," he began. "One Christmas Eve she knocked on my door and handed it to me, all stitched with her beautiful embroidery. I thought I'd wear it for her today."

Sobs were heard throughout the church. Yet, each person found the strength to get through their part, whether singing or reading or dancing, as if Pat were holding them together when they needed it most.

"Pat was a brilliant gal," the homily began, "and she could have used her genius to get rich, to make it to the very top of the ladder. And believe me when I say this gal could have. Instead, she chose to serve others, to use her mind, her genius, for serving the Lord."

"One day," he continued, putting his hands in his pockets, a sure sign that a story would follow, "Pat went walking through the woods picking berries. She filled her bowl to overflowing and was ready to come home. But she met a man with an empty bowl who was very hungry and he asked her if she'd trade with him. Without a moment's hesitation she gave the man her full bowl and took the empty one. What Pat didn't realize was the bowl he gave her was made of pure gold. And that was the bowl she held out time and time again for each of us. . . ."

The story ended, capturing Pat's life so beautifully, to be followed by words of reality, words heard only at funeral services. "Welcome your servant, Patricia," Father told Jesus. It was an easy picture to envision. Pat standing before Jesus with that beautiful smile, the one she had worn for each of us.

Pat had no need for words. No need for explanations or rationalizations. She met Jesus with the only valid, true confession of one's life, "Who do my friends say that I am?"

The Purple Heart

ONE NAME AFTER ANOTHER WAS CALLED. AND EACH IN turn the soldiers marched in step to receive their medals of honor. They humbly bowed their heads as the medal was hung around their neck. The last name was called and the applause that broke out was thunderous. When the room returned to silence, they read the names of the men who had died for the cause. The mothers cried, but were filled with pride for their sons who had given up their lives.

Suddenly a mother stood up. "Sir," she said, "I am afraid my son's name has been omitted from your list. He, too, has given his life for the sake of peace."

The general was visibly shaken at such an oversight. "Please accept our sincere apology," he told her. "This will be corrected immediately. What division did your son serve in?" he asked.

"I'm sorry if you misunderstood," she said. "My son did not fight in the war. He was a conscientious objector and died for that cause. I am here in behalf of his purple heart."

The general could hardly control his outrage. He had to talk loudly to be heard above the jeers of the crowd. "This room's for heroes, madam, not cowards who run from their duty. If you know what's good for you, you had better leave right now, and don't ever show your face around here again."

Tears filled the mother's eyes. She thought of her son. The general grabbed her by the arm and escorted her out of the room. Once again, Mary was led away from the scene of the crucifixion.

Food in my Father's House

PERHAPS YOU HAVE HEARD THE STATEMENT; ONE THIRD OF the world is on a diet while the other third starves. Christians cannot dismiss this statement as part of today's news. We, as believers, cannot truly share Our Lord's body and blood while ignoring the very heart of His Words summarized so beautifully in Matthew's Gospel account: "Lord, when did we see you hungry or thirsty or away from home or naked or ill or in prison and not attend you in your needs?" He will answer them, I assure you, "as often as you neglected to do it to one of these least ones, you neglected to do it to me."

Through some mystery, all of us here are dieters. We live in a land of plenty. We don't want people to starve. In fact, we are moved to compassion, even to anger that this injustice can happen when God created the world with enough food to provide for all of His children. There is no doubt in my mind that each one of us would feed these people given the opportunity. Wanting to is the first part. How to is the challenge. Is it reality to believe we can live the Gospel message or is it just an ideal?

For years my husband and I searched for that answer: how to. Then a program was introduced at our church that answered our search. It gave us the inner peace we could not have until we could feel we were living the Words of Christ, not just hearing them. The program is called sacrificial giving. The idea is so very simple: give back to the Lord a part of all He has given to your family. This then becomes your return gift to the Lord. The gift is called tithing. Tithing is as old as the Old Testament when people gave 10% of their harvest back to the Lord. In that tradition and also the spirit of the New Testament, 10% is still suggested as our gift today. Not being familiar with tithing, we were a little shocked to hear such an amount. Ten percent from our gross pay certainly represents a large sum. Realistically, few families, including ours, can immediately begin to give 10% of their pay. But what it meant to us, was actually thinking about what we were giving. Sitting down and planning our Sunday gift. All these years we gave out of habit. The habit was developed when we were children going to church with our parents on Sunday. I hate to say that was over twenty years ago. Two dollars then represented a sacrifice to our parents. Today, it won't even buy one soda and a box of popcorn at the theatre. My father often talks about what a nickel could buy in his days. And it seems strange to think we made the connection with inflation in every aspect of our lives except church. The important thing, however, was that once we made the connection, we did something about it. We sat down at the kitchen table and decided on an amount that represented a sacrifice. It wasn't ten percent. That amount has to be worked up to. The main thing is to make a commitment; one you will live with every week, no matter what. This commitment is to truly be a sacrifice. For the first time in our lives we were placing God above our bills. We were developing a trust relationship with Him. And, as always, we found Him true to His word: Seek first his kingship over you, his way of holiness and all these things will be given you besides. As much as we gave to church, and this amount has increased each of the four years we have been tithing, we never seemed to have less. In fact, giving away part of what we have has allowed us for the first time to fully enjoy that which is left.

Our change in giving brought about many other changes—one being our attitude concerning envelopes. Let's face it, a habit requires no thought, and as such usually no feeling. When we gave out of habit, the basket had no feelings connected to it. On the other hand, our tithe, our return gift to the Lord, has great meaning. This is a well-thought-out gift—hand-picked for the Lord. We want to wrap it. To remember it is part of our prayer, not an obligation, rather an expression of the joy we feel in giving our present to the guest of honor at our Sunday banquet—Our Lord.

Most of the families in our community experienced these same feelings. The envelopes became a bond between us. We felt a closeness growing. We were all in this same boat together, paddling hard, real hard, but enjoying the ride twice as much as we began to understand where we were going.

Sacrificial giving gave us a new awareness of what church means. Before, church was a place we went to. Now church is a place that belongs to us, it is us. Jesus carefully chose the church as the place his believers would gather to share the bread, to share the word, but also, through the community of believers, bring His words to action. It is our responsibility to keep our place of worship alive and well-tended, physically as well as spiritually. Tithing was the answer to our prayers of how to live the Gospel message. When we were searching, we felt overwhelmed that Jesus was saying, okay, you feed the poor of the world. When we realized, through the scriptures presented in sacrificial giving, that Jesus instituted the church for that purpose, we no longer felt overwhelmed. That message is stated plainly in Malachi. "Bring the whole tithe into the storehouse, that there may be food in my house, and try me in this, says the Lord of hosts: Shall I not open for you the flood-gates of heaven, to pour down blessing upon you without measure?" That message is again stated clearly in the Acts of the Apostles: "The community of believers were of one heart and one mind. None of them ever claimed anything as his own: rather everything was held in common . . . nor, was there anyone needy among them, for all who owned property or houses sold them and donated the proceeds. They used to lay the gifts at the feet of the apostles to be distributed to everyone according to his needs." The tithe is always mentioned with the community of believers in mind. It is obvious that part of the tithe must go for the upkeep of the church building and the great expense it takes to run it. But how much more important is the second directive of the tithe, to care for the orphan, the widow, the stranger, the foreigner among us.

The best feeling that has come from our sacrificial giving is no longer feeling we are two people trying to live the Gospel message alone. We are no longer two people trying to feed one third of the world. We have experienced the difference that can be made by a community of believers who make the commitment to place God first in their lives by returning 10% of all He has given to our families.

And through the instrument of church and the concept of tithing, we begin to understand anew the miracle of the multiplication of the loaves and fishes.

"Where ever your treasure lies, there shall you find your heart."

—Matthew 6:21

SHE WALKED INTO THE COMMUNITY MENTAL HEALTH CENTER with our tithing check. "This is a donation from the families of our church community," she said. The woman looked at the check and was visibly surprised at the amount. The check reflected the sacrifice and commitment of families who put God first in their life.

"I think we'd better give this to the director," she said. They went to his office and handed him the check. "This is a donation from their church," the woman repeated. He opened the check and was completely amazed. "This is from a church?" he asked. "Yes," she answered. "Why are you so surprised?"

"To be perfectly honest," he said, "I didn't think churches got involved with social concerns." Their program will house young adults who are not able to live with their families. Somehow, those words seem too mild to reflect what that really means. Counseling and training for independent living will be provided.

He was very interested in our church. They talked for some time. He wanted to know our concerns for the poor. She told him about our sacrificial giving program. How each family makes a weekly commitment that allows us to tithe monthly to many places. He couldn't believe that 20% of all our income goes directly to the poor.

In fact, for the entire day the word church was heard throughout the Community Health Center. One woman said she was going to ask her priest that very week what their church was doing for the poor. A man said this was enough to make him think about going back to church again. Some shook their heads and said they thought the church had moved away from the poor.

It was a strange thing. We went to the Community Mental Health Center with one purpose—to help the poor. And then we watched as each person there received "just the amount" they too needed from our tithing check. . . .

Barnraisings

PEOPLE STILL TALK OF THE BARNRAISINGS OF YESTERDAY. People coming from all directions to lend a hand, men swinging hammers, women bringing bakings of bread. And before sundown a barn stands against the blue expanse of sky.

People wistfully talk of the barnraisings of yesterday as if it were a time gone by. Yet, in a real sense, we, as church, continue to raise "barn" after "barn" together. Every Sunday morning people come from all directions to lend a hand. They carry the hammer and nails and bakings of bread in the small white envelope each family brings. And before sundown many "barns" have been raised and can be seen against the blue expanse of God's sky.

Perhaps that is part of the special feelings we share at church, as our families come together for the "barnraisings"!

The Well

WORDS ARE NOT ENOUGH TO DESCRIBE THE FEELINGS WE HAVE come to know. In searching for the words, a very simple picture came to mind—the picture of a well. The picture of feeling so thirsty and dry and looking for a place that offered some water. And we came to church and found a well. Other families were already at the well, and seeing us arrive, they gladly lowered the bucket, and drew that refreshing water. Here, they said, drink until your thirst is gone.

The well became a restful place, a place that offered contentment. And each week there was a thirst that drew us to return to the well; for this thirst could only be quenched there. And we couldn't imagine any better feeling than drinking from the well. Until one day, we were asked to draw the bucket for someone else who was coming.

How simple it seems now going from family to community, going from the feeling of it being enough to drink from the well to the joy of drawing the bucket for another who comes. And now, as community, we have found an even greater joy: drawing from our well and actually bringing our "water" to others who thirst.

The water we bring is in the form of food, shelter and clothing. It is education and training for a better way of life. It is hope in the form of seeds and agricultural tools. It is experiencing people who believe in Jesus and feeling how powerful this Jesus must be to not only have touched them, but to have moved them to action. It is drawing the bucket for people who are also dry and thirsty but could not find a well.

A church well operates on love and friendship. It is kept full by sacrificial giving. The water flows from each family who has made the decision to return to Our Lord a part of all He has given to their families. This weekly commitment keeps our well from running dry. It allows us to say some beautiful words, "O let all who thirst, let them come to the water. . . ."

Enter by the Narrow Gate

WE ARE ALL TRAVELING ON A JOURNEY THROUGH THIS lifetime. Most people choose the highway. It is straight and well paved. It takes only a matter of seconds to get accustomed to the speed. And in no time at all, you've arrived at the conclusion that you are going too fast to stop for anything that might cross your path. It's you and the road directly ahead, getting someplace fast. There is only one danger—missing your exit!

Welcome to the back road! It is not only winding but goes uphill. It usually leads to places that are not written on the map. (Why are those places always the most beautiful?) All along the way are breathtaking scenes. Suddenly you no longer feel in such a hurry to get somewhere, as you begin to see that where you are is pretty beautiful too.

Sacrificial giving is a journey on the back road. It is a hard road to travel, especially the weeks when the "repair bills" come in. And it is always tempting to jump back in the fast lane, just for a while, you promise yourself. There we don't have to keep stopping for others by giving our weekly commitment, our return gift to the Lord.

But the "view" we've seen on the back road, the promise it's given of what still lies ahead makes our journey too wondrous to turn back. Welcome to the back road!

One Thorn at a Time

WE HAD JUST REACHED THE TENTH STATION OF THE CROSS—Jesus is stripped of His garments. He looked especially vulnerable at that moment, wearing the image of the whip so plainly across His flesh with the crown of thorns piercing His beautiful face. Everyone was lost for words except a quiet young girl praying the stations near her mother. Suddenly such an exciting thought came to her that even her own shyness could not hold back the words. "You know how at Christmas time," she began, as if speaking directly to Jesus on the Cross, "if we've done a good deed, we get to put a piece of hay in the manger. And if we've been very good until Christmas, Jesus has a warm soft bed to lie in? Well, couldn't we do the same thing for Lent? We could pretend that every time we did a good deed we were taking one of the thorns out of Jesus' crown. . . ."

How different the experience of Lent is in our lives today. No longer a time to deny ourselves, but rather a time to find ourselves to give to others. Perhaps what we find hardly seems enough to make a difference. But that is seeing ourselves through our own eyes!

There are many ways your family can make a difference through sacrificial giving—reaching into yourselves for others. Sometimes the only way to dismantle a "crown of thorns" is removing them one at a time.

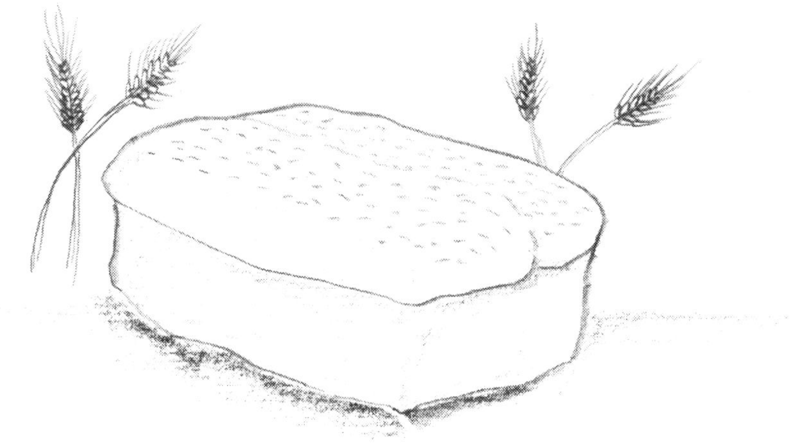

The Bread of Life

A STALK OF WHEAT WAS GROWING GOLDEN IN THE SUNshine. It waited for the farmer's whistle. It became a part of the child, resting his cheek on the warmth of the cow during milking. It watched the garden answer the sun's call with its greenness. It felt love growing.

And, understanding love for the first time, wanted to return it. In so doing, it looked upon itself and saw such smallness there. It was not enough for even one small loaf of bread. The farmer's whistle, sounding the same to the ears, seemed to sound different to the heart. It carried the sound of not being able to return all the love and gifts you feel were given to you.

The sun continued to rise and the wheat continued to grow until, one day, it touched the wheat growing around it. The wheat was standing closely together, almost as if holding hands, and the stalk of wheat could no longer see itself, having become so much a part of the field.

Slowly, beautifully, the farmer's whistle rang out clear across the field, and so happily, the stalk of wheat could suddenly see all the bread that together they would bring the farmer.

Sacrificial giving sows the field. It provides the harvest through which the church community can feed His poor.

Finding the Real Christmas Presence

IT TAKES A FEW MINUTES TO REALIZE THE HOUSE IS QUIET. The television is shut off. The kids are in bed. For a few precious moments you can look at the lights and quietly remember. It all comes back, the old living room, the young faces, the feelings.

The lights glow softly. A little girl's face comes to mind. You can almost see her unwrapping that doll, sobbing and holding onto her, asking again, "is she really mine?" How is it possible a child never had a present before?

The winds shake the house. You wrap your clothes tighter and try to picture the faces of the homeless. You are glad they are part of your family now.

Faces from the mission in Appalachia drift in under the tree. That woman expecting her eighth child. Her husband died in a car crash. She has one thin dime in her pocketbook. But the sister knocks on her door and gives her a present from our community, from our tithing money. The present will keep her family going for a month. She can't believe it!

The woman with ten children; two blind in a school many miles away; one hemophiliac. She shyly asks for gas money to be able to visit her children once a month. She unwraps the present from our church family.

A family in Haiti celebrating Christmas by throwing away their bug-infested mats and for the first time in their lives, buying new cotton ones, a present from us. And she remembers how they wrote that they never thought they would live to see such a rich Christmas.

So many faces reflected in the soft glow of the lights.

Suddenly the room looks different. What was the trouble, you think. The worry. The expense. The rush disappears. You don't know how it happened, it always comes when you least expect; the moment when He allows you to open the real "presence" of Christmas!

A Shred of Light

TWENTY-FIVE PEOPLE WERE THERE FOR THE PEACE VIGIL held in the center of town. They stood in a circle, their hands and faces wrapped securely against the cold. Three lit candles flickered on the ground in the middle of them. Hand-made signs displayed what was in their hearts: "Pray for Peace," "Give Peace a Chance," and a simple white dove painted on a black cardboard. They held hands and prayed the *Our Father*. They said the *Angelus*. They believed in the power of prayer. Yet, in the dark vastness of the starry night sky, they indeed felt an overwhelming sense of smallness. Many people offered a prayer and for a moment all was still. Unexpectedly, a quiet woman in the group began to speak. "This might sound trivial," she began with some hesitation, "but I would like to share something that happened to me during the past week. I was washing a batch of dark clothes. And when I took them out of the washing machine, I couldn't believe that, once again, a tissue had escaped my attention. Now I was sure I had checked all the pockets. What amazed me was that one tiny tissue had managed to affect that whole batch of clothes. Not one piece of clothing in the whole load of wash was left untouched. And as I was standing here, feeling quite overwhelmed with the thought of a handful of people making a difference, well, suddenly that tiny tissue popped into my mind. I just wanted to share the feeling with you," she finished shyly.

"I like that idea," a man in the group said. "We're a little bit of white clinging to the dark."

"Isn't it always the smallest things that can cause the most problems?" a young boy remarked thoughtfully.

"Why, I've left a tissue in a pocket a hundred times," a woman said, laughing. "I know just what you're talking about. And the worst part of it is, that no matter how much you try, you can never really get the tissue off the clothes entirely. Some of it always manages to stick."

They were all laughing now. "I don't get it," the priest joked. "You mean you purposely leave a Kleenex in your pocket. . . ."

"Never mind," the woman said, putting her arm around his and winking at the woman who told the story. "That's one sermon you won't hear until women are ordained!"